It's Not Where You
START,
But Where You
FINISH
That COUNTS

REVEREND CHARLES W. QUANN

WESTBOW
PRESS®
A DIVISION OF THOMAS NELSON
& ZONDERVAN

Scripture quotations are taken from the Holy Bible, New Living Translation, copyright ©1996, 2004, 2007, 2013, 2015 by Tyndale House Foundation. Used by permission of Tyndale House Publishers, Inc., Carol Stream, Illinois 60188. All rights reserved.

WestBow Press books may be ordered through booksellers or by contacting:

WestBow Press
A Division of Thomas Nelson & Zondervan
1663 Liberty Drive
Bloomington, IN 47403
www.westbowpress.com
1 (866) 928-1240

ISBN: 978-1-5127-6888-6 (sc)
ISBN: 978-1-5127-6890-9 (hc)
ISBN: 978-1-5127-6889-3 (e)

Library of Congress Control Number: 2016920873

Print information available on the last page.

WestBow Press rev. date: 3/15/2017

Contents

Foreword

T o some it may seem like a high form of flattery to be asked to write the foreword for a sensitive and revealing document of this kind. That isn't the case in this instance.

To me, being asked to write a few words prior to the publishing of this book is both an honor and a privilege. That is because what I know about the author as a person and preacher/pastor not only humbles me but also warrants a level of modesty and honesty on my part to do justice to him as well as to all potential readers. Indeed, it means that since he was licensed and ordained to the Christian ministry under my pastorate, I must take some credit or blame for what he has become (or hasn't become) at this significant state in his growth and development.

Readers will soon discover, therefore, in every word and phrase, in every sentence and paragraph, the genuine effort on the part of the author to be as transparent as possible. In addition, what the author says discloses the integrity of one who genuinely feels that the written exposure of himself in this fashion (at whatever risk) may be encouraging and helpful to all of us who dare claim to be exponents of the gospel of Jesus Christ and caretakers of the members of His kingdom here on earth.

I strongly encourage every reader and potential reader of this testimonial to read it with empathy and understanding of where he has come from and what he has come through.

Read it and be blessed. Read it and be enlightened. Read it and be inspired. Read it with compassion and be lifted to a new level of appreciation of what God can do through and with a life committed to the divine service of the people of God as well as to the worship of the most high God, our Creator, made known to the world in Jesus Christ.

Pastor Albert Franklin Campbell, Pastor Emeritus
Mt. Carmel Baptist Church, Philadelphia

Foreword

If there is one narrative that unites Jews and African-Americans, it is the biblical exodus from Egypt. Most of us remember Moses standing up to Pharaoh and declaring, "Let my people go." These words have inspired both of our peoples on their journey to freedom.

But after the Israelites left Egypt, the work really began. God brought the plagues, but the people had to march. Along their way through the desert, the Israelites confronted enemies (Amalek), internal rebellion (Korach), and internal dissent (the golden calf). But they also experienced profound moments of faith and triumph. They overcame overwhelming obstacles as they crossed the Red Sea and experienced the dawning of redemption at Mount Sinai, where they covenanted with God.

Likewise, my friend Pastor Quann received a call from God to minister to his community. The call began his journey, which has brought tremendous hardship, loss, and personal defeat. He has suffered for his faith and courageously stood up, even when the forces against him were at times overwhelming. But thankfully, he has also tasted the sweetness of community, friendship, faith, and love. He has courageously transformed his church, with a long history in the African-American community, into a multicultural church celebrating diversity and mutual respect. Under his leadership, Bethlehem Baptist Church humbly "loves God and serves people."

The Hebrew Bible is full of dramatic events, such as the parting of the Red Sea, the covenant at Sinai, and of course the creation stories of Genesis. For me, however, the most dramatic event is near the end of Deuteronomy. Moses called heaven and earth to bear witness to his vision. He called upon his people to remember their past, celebrate their present, and look with hope to their future. Moses called out, "My doctrine shall drop as the rain, my speech shall distill as the dew; as the small rain upon the tender grass, and the showers upon the herb, I will proclaim the name of the Lord; and ascribe greatest unto our God." Charles's words and actions have penetrated not only our community but, more importantly, our hearts. The pastor has taught us all to fight despair, to hope against all odds, and of course to "walk in the Light of the Lord."

Pastor Quann, like Moses, has shepherded his community and brought about a deeper faith, a more resolute commitment to the poor and social justice. There is no doubt Moses suffered for his stances. God wouldn't let him enter the Promised Land, but Moses wouldn't waver. Despite the pain and pitfalls of his journey, Pastor Quann has emerged stronger, wiser, and, most importantly, kinder. He won't waver. I will always remember his greatest lesson to me. He said to me on a particularly dark day, "Hardship can make us bitter, or it can make us better. I want to be better."

At the time of this writing, both Jews and African-Americans are confronting a renewal of bigotry and hatred. We see it on the streets of Europe and Ferguson. Partly because of my friendship with Pastor Quann and the lessons he has taught me, I see Ferguson—and now Baltimore—with ever-increased empathy and the need for justice. I know and am grateful that he appreciates the pain of the Jewish community as well.

One of my greatest gifts is to have been part of this pastor's journey. We have learned together. We gave grown together, and I know that my faith is stronger for having been a part of his spiritual pilgrimage. Because of him, so many others who know and love him and I are indeed "better."

For this, I will always be thankful.

Rabbi Gregory S. Marx,
Congregation Beth Or, Maple Glen, Pa.

Acknowledgments

It is with gratitude to God that I acknowledge the many people who have been part of my life story, many of whom appear in this book. I would like to acknowledge my wife, Tanya, and my sons, daughters, and grandchildren. Last but not least, I would like to recognize my chief of staff Brenda Benson, who has spent hours—and I do mean hours—by helping, writing, listening, and praying as we worked together to produce this first edition.

Introduction

We serve an amazing God. The blessings God gives us in our lives are so numerous we cannot even begin to count them or even name them all. I know I'm not alone when I say that God has richly blessed us. This book is about the blessings almighty God has given to me. I need to put a disclaimer in this introduction about the book's title. It's really not about me at all but rather about where God has brought me. Let me add: it's not about serving in some high position in the corporate world, having a large congregation, accumulating a lot of wealth, or living large. Rather, it's about how your life can be a blessing.

This book is for ordinary people upon whom God can grant favor. In these pages, you will see the hand of God in every aspect of my life—through the pain and shame, through the misfortunes—and learn that God is still active and working on my behalf. Even when I wasn't aware of the power and presence of God, He was using some experiences to develop my faith, character, and trust in Him. As I reflect on my life, I realize more and more the profound meaning of Romans 8:28: "And we know that God causes everything to work together for the good of those who love God and are called according to his purpose for them". I must admit that some of the things that took place in my life I really didn't see as good, but God used them and is still using them.

God inspired me to write this book because I am well aware that there are many in our society whose lives were nearly in ruins during their early childhood. In fact, I know there are many people who have shared their life story, and their pain was far greater than mine. As

African-Americans, we know about pain and suffering, and we see the evidence of destruction all around us. We live in neighborhoods full of crime, violence, and self-destruction. We have watched our educational system fail us and seen the government turn its back on us. This isn't true with just African-Americans; other minorities face the same plight. The poor, elderly, and disadvantaged begin their lives in despair. But hopefully, regardless of where you have started, you will know that where you begin doesn't have to be where you will end.

As you read this book prayerfully, perhaps you will take the time to review your own life and see how some of those unfortunate circumstances have caused you to rely more on God. This book would never have been written without some of those painful experiences, and I wouldn't be the man God has caused me to be without having gone through some difficult days. We cannot allow our past to prevent us from moving forward; if anything, the past can be the foundation of a new beginning. This story isn't simply a journey about my years of pastoring, even though some of those days have been difficult. Rather, it's about me as a husband, father, and grandfather; and it shows how the mercy of God has shaped and cultivated my life.

You don't need to be preacher, pastor, educator, or political leader to be able to appreciate where God has taken you. All you have to do is be aware of the power and presence of God and how He transforms lives. I have come to love butterflies because they represent new beginnings. Think about how a butterfly can emerge from a cocoon and become a beautiful reflection of God's changing and amazing grace. When we first look at the Cacoon, we are unable to see beauty until the butterfly emerges and comes forth; it represents new life. That's the beauty of God. He can take some of the dirt and soil in our lives, and make a radical change, thus giving us new hopes, dreams, and aspirations. Never allow the past to determine your future and use every day for the glory of God.

Please do not mistake my explaining for complaining. What I'm writing aren't complaints but illustrations and examples of how God can turn things around. It's so easy to complain or give excuses for why we are where we are. I would strongly argue that far too many people blame others for their plight or give excuses about how bad their childhood was. As someone so wisely said, "Get over it." Most of us have had some things happen in our lives that may not have been fair, but we received God's favor. Don't dwell on what was unfair but rather focus on the goodness of God.

I pray that those who read this book will find encouragement and strength to move beyond their past, that they will grab hold of the future and begin to have the courage and strength to change those things in their lives that cause them so much misery. I firmly believe we have a choice. We can go to a pity party, stay there, and dwell on all the things that have happened in our lives, or we can decide we want a new way of life.

Life started slowly for me, but I picked up momentum along the way, with the help of God and the people He has placed in my life. "Life is a journey and the race is not given to the swift but to those who endure to the end" (Eccl. 9:11). I'm compelled to add another disclaimer at this point, because in no way does the title of this book indicate or imply that I'm at the finishing point. The race isn't over, and I still have a lot of living to do. That's the point I want to make. I'm looking for God to do some new and exciting things in my marriage and as a father, pastor, and servant of God, for I believe the best is yet to come.

This is just a snapshot of what has taken place at this point and for years to come, for I plan to write a second edition. This first edition is more about the starting point and where I am now—all because of the grace of God. He alone deserves the glory and honor. May you be inspired by what God has done not only for me but also for the countless others who have started lagging behind. Never give up on anyone, for God can take those born in despair and move them to the mountain of hope.

Follow me as I take you through the paths of my life from early childhood to present time. Track God in your own life and see whether there is any resemblance between my journey and yours. Maybe this may not pertain to you, but perhaps there are those in your family or circle of friends who can relate to the hand of God moving in their lives. Maybe you've heard a testimony of how someone overcame an obstacle or burden as the result of God's hand of mercy. Be prepared to share with someone who may be caught in a web and cannot find a way out; and tell him or her about the goodness of God and about how He can turn any life around. Read to be inspired, to be challenged, and to acknowledge the powerful hand of God, for it is no secret what God is able to do. What He has done for me He will do for others too.

Learn to trust and depend on Him, for there is no failure in God. "For I can do everything through Christ who gives me strength". (Philippians 4:13). We have the capacity to overcome every burden and care life brings our way. Be blessed as you read through these pages, and may God strengthen you in your daily walk.

Chapter 1

My Early Childhood

O ne of the greatest blessings God grants us is that of memory, and I realize now more than ever that it is a precious gift. Many in our society of all ages have experienced Alzheimer's and suffered the inability to recall many of the rich experiences in their lives. I wrote this chapter not only from my heart but also from the priceless gift of memory.

I was born as the second of three children, the middle child. I have one sister, who is one year older, and one younger sister, who is now deceased. Being the only boy in the family, I was told how spoiled I was many times; of course, I don't remember that. I grew up in an urban area and in a mixed block of Italians and African-Americans; we were one of the few African-American families on the block. There was nothing lavish about our home; it was a simple five-room home with a kitchen, dining room, living room, and two bedrooms. The street I lived on I now refer to as Home Place, and it was lined with trees. In fact, we had a large tree in front of our home, and it stood for many years until a hurricane came and knocked it down. That tree provided a lot of shade for us during the hot summers.

We lived between two Italian families, and I must admit that I knew little to nothing about racial prejudice. In fact, I remember running in and out of their homes and sitting on the steps with them; there were white marble steps I had to wash as I grew older. Those days were full of blessings as the neighbors shared their resources with us. I enjoyed the Italian meals they prepared; they would sometimes bring spaghetti and ravioli to our home on Sunday afternoons.

One Italian family across the street from us had a death in their home; they put crape on the door, and the body was brought to the house and placed in the living room. I remember going in to see it and running out with tears in my eyes, for I had never experienced anything quite like that. It was my first encounter with death. I soon discovered it was a tradition to have the body in the living room, and I was assured that there was nothing for me to be fearful about. That event made a lasting impression on my life.

My mother did the day's work of cleaning the homes of middle-class families. She also worked for many years in a department store, which no longer exists, as well as in a restaurant, all to help put food on our table. I don't remember too much about my father other than the fact that I was told he was part Cherokee Indian. I have a vivid remembrance of my grandmother, his mother; she had long hair that hung down her back.

I'm not sure what age I was, but I was old enough to know there was tension in our home. My mother and father were always arguing. At an early age I learned about prayer, since I had heard my grandmother speak about the power of it. I didn't really know how to pray, but I asked God for peace in our home. I disliked the confusion and turmoil, but there was little I could do to change them. I often longed to hear the words "I love you," but that was seldom said. I didn't believe then that God would provide me with an opportunity later in my life to release myself from some of the pain.

I have learned in life that some events happen that aren't fair, but in spite of them, God always blesses. We cannot dwell on what is unfair; rather, we must focus only on God's goodness. We cannot continue to give excuses about how bad our childhood was or how we missed out on love. Most of us have had things happen in our lives that weren't so good, but we cannot live in the past—we must move forward. I firmly believe we have a choice; we can decide that we want a new way of life.

My grandmother lived with us for as long as I can remember and was the matriarch of our family. I believe she was born in a different part of the state, and she, along with my mother, moved to the inner city. She affectionately gave me the nickname, Buddy, and it's one my family still calls me today. She was crippled and did ironing for the neighbors to help provide food for our family. She was a great cook and did most of the cooking and cleaning in our house. Our Sunday meals were the blessing of the week, and I looked forward to having chicken, sweet potatoes, and greens—and the leftovers were so good on Mondays. During the week we ate our meals in the kitchen, and on Sundays we ate in the dining room. One of my favorites was my grandmother's apple pie, which she made from applesauce.

When we gathered for our Sunday dinner, my grandmother would lead us in prayer. I never remember her attending church, but I do remember her singing hymns and praising God throughout the house. She was a woman of great faith and believed God would supply the blessings we needed. I never saw her get angry or complain; she simply gave of herself freely and willingly. She always made a fuss over me, holding me close to her bosom and making me laugh. My sisters always told me I was her favorite, which was probably true; she loved me, and I loved her dearly. My love for her was so deep, and she loved me with all her heart. I often speak of her and give God thanks for her, as she was a significant force in my life. I don't remember anything at all about my grandfather; he was never mentioned, and he never lived with us and played very little part in our lives

Because our home had only two bedrooms, I slept with my grandmother while my two sisters shared a room with my mother. Not having my own room, I had to share a closet with my sisters. I had very few clothes, so I didn't need a lot of space. Whenever I put a hole in my pants, my grandmother would patch them so I could wear them again. I even had to put cardboard in my shoes when I got a hole in them because we couldn't afford to buy another pair.

I never received an allowance, but I did have ways of getting a little money. Whenever it snowed, I would shovel our pavement and our neighbors' walks as well. The neighbor would give me a little money for shoveling; sometimes I didn't tell my grandmother, because she would have told me to give it back. Sometimes after shoveling, a few of the neighbors would make snow cream by mixing the snow with vanilla and sugar; that would be our treat for the day. I loved the snow because the schools would close, and I could stay home and look out the window at the streets piled with it. The snowplows never came through our little street, so the snow would sometimes last days before it would melt. The neighbors would all work together to plow out those who had a car; we didn't have one, but I always helped them dig their cars out.

At an early age, I was hospitalized for a period of time because I had scarlet fever. It was a very lonely time because I was isolated from others, and I even missed an entire year of school. Our home was quarantined, and the hospital put a sign on the front door, indicating someone inside was very ill. This was a hard time for me; I would pull the skin off my hands, arms, and face. My grandmother told me the doctors had informed her that I wouldn't have a fruitful life, but as you can see, God had other plans. They also said I could possibly have some restrictions in my life, but my grandmother assured me that God was going to allow me to live a full and meaningful life.

She wasn't well educated, but she knew about the power of God and relied on Him. That's the way she handled everything—by trusting God. She would often tell me not only how much she loved me but also how much God loved me. She didn't just say this, but her actions proved it. My grandmother was my rock, and I found in her a love that cannot be described. As a result of her life, I have grown to the point to be able to handle many of life's problems, as she never dwelled on the negative but always focused on the positive. There were many times when she defended me when she heard others criticize me and say unkind things about me. She never wanted to hear any words from anyone that would cause me pain. She would always speak up and say, "That's my boy."

I'll never forget when we got our first television—it was a joyous day. We were probably one of the last families on our block to acquire one, but no one was more grateful than we were. The television was considered a piece of furniture that added to our living room, and we were so proud. On Sunday evenings we would all sit around together and watch *The Ed Sullivan Show* and other family programs. One show my mother and grandmother really loved was *I Remember Mama*. They would often cry when they watched this show.

My sisters and I had a good relationship while growing up. We each had our chores to do, and those started at an early age; mine was washing dishes twice a week. I always pouted when it was my turn; my grandmother scolded me, and I washed them reluctantly. We had an icebox, and I was responsible for emptying the water and had to make sure the water wouldn't run over in the pan. Sometimes I would mess up, and water would run over on the floor; boy, did I hear it. Besides checking the water under the icebox, I was also responsible for banking the fire. I would shift the coal so we could use it over again; then I pulled out the coal that was completely burned and saved the coal we could reuse.

I went to an elementary school in my neighborhood, where my first learning took place. I recently learned it was one of the schools that recently closed and is now a condominium. My sisters and I would walk to school together every day, because it was only a few blocks from our home. There were just a few students of color in the school at that time. After school, I would rush home because I enjoyed playing in the street—that is, until my grandmother would come to the door and call loudly, "Come in here." Her voice rang out throughout the whole block. After dinner, I knew it was time to do my homework. There were times I felt sad, especially when there were events at school my parents couldn't attend because of my mother's work schedule. I had a rough time, because I was often teased about my skin color and for having curly hair; they didn't call it "bullying" then as we do now, but I was teased. I was somewhat timid and very insecure; therefore, I was made fun of and called names. The treatment was hurtful and painful, but I managed to survive.

There was a couple who lived across the street and didn't have children of their own. I would run into their home just like I was their child; they also became part of my life. You will notice throughout this book how many people have impacted my life. They weren't a biological part of my family, but God placed them in my life for a reason. I believe with all my heart that nothing happens by accident or chance but by the providence of God.

Christmas was always a special time in our home. We loved coming downstairs early Christmas morning to see what was under the tree. It was my favorite holiday, because that was when I received most of my new clothes. The neighbors gave me many of the clothes I had. I didn't know anything about secondhand clothes; I just wore them with such pride. Along with new clothes, I did receive a few toys. How I longed for Santa. It was a good time for me and my sisters, because we had extra food, fruit, and a cardboard fireplace from the five- and ten-cent store, where we hung three stockings, one for each of us. We were told that if we were bad, the stockings would be filled with coal. A couple of years I did get coal in my socking, but I always got a nice little gift along with the coal. Another tradition was that there was always a joyous spirit during the holiday; in fact, the neighbors would go in and out of each other's homes and fellowship throughout the day.

There are so many memories lodged in my heart; I probably will think of many more after I complete this book. In the next chapter, I talk about my middle years.

Chapter 2

My Middle Years

After completing the sixth grade, I attended junior high school in my neighborhood. I could look right out my front door and see the school. At the end of the school day, I was happy to hear the school bell ring and get home in about five minutes because I loved to play in the street when I got home from school. I often forgot to do my homework, so my grandmother continually challenged me about getting it done and rewarded me when I bought home good grades on my papers. I was so excited about attending junior high school, but that didn't last long for I was faced with many obstacles and challenges. It was an integrated school with both black and white students. Still being insecure, shy, and timid, I encountered bullying. I was just an average student, and my grades were far from good, but I was determined to improve them and become involved in some after-school activities. On several occasions I tried to make the junior varsity baseball team but was never successful.

My home was still very chaotic, but it was home. I spent a good deal of time with an older couple, who were no relation to me. I called them the affectionate names, Sugar and Anna Mae. They were dear to my heart because they came into my life and showered me with such great love. They lived about six blocks from my home in a three-story home, called an "ace deuce," which consisted of one room on each floor. They had a wood stove for heat, which warmed their living room, the bedroom on the second floor, and a bedroom on the third floor, where I slept. They never owned a TV; they simply had a radio we would listen to. Their icebox was kept in the shed, and they had an outhouse behind their home.

Sugar was crippled, and when he worked, I would meet him at his job when he got off on Friday and spend the weekend with them. They would spoil me all weekend and buy me my favorite sweets. They weren't religious, and I don't remember them having many friends, yet in spite of their meager home, I always felt welcome and loved. There were no arguments or nasty words heard in their home. After Sugar retired from his job, he would get a check once a month, and he and Anna Mae would have someone drive them to New Jersey, where they would spend the entire day relaxing. While I was with them, I simply enjoyed the day by putting money in the jukebox and listening to music. This outing was their enjoyment in life, and I didn't judge them for that. The more I think about it, the more I realize it was their one outlet to escape the reality of poverty and pain. My visits with them lasted for several years until they got sick; she passed away first, and he lived alone until he died several years later.

I continued my studies in junior high school and was able to make several friends who were true and loyal. Several of them were from really nice homes, and when I visited them, I always left, feeling envious. Their homes were modestly furnished, but beyond that, they had two parents. I watched how their mother and father expressed love to one another, and I heard words I had never heard in my own home. In some cases I even became resentful, because I didn't have the same warmth in our home. The need to belong became great, and I yearned for it every day. I often became moody and cold when I was home, and I even found myself acting rude at times.

Eventually, this problem carried over into school, and my report card reflected a lack of study, discipline, and respect. My grades began to decline, and I felt no one really cared about me. There was one teacher, Mr. Jones, who really took an interest in me. He told me on more than one occasion that I could do better than what my grades reflected. I felt his sincerity, because he didn't say this with harshness but rather with soft words. His caring words really helped me, if only temporarily, to try harder. The harder I tried to improve my grades and be accepted by some of my peers, the more difficult it became. My insecurity didn't help. I was light skinned and had curly hair, which made me a target for so many unkind words and deeds.

I remember getting into a fight with someone who constantly bullied me. His torment of me increased because of a girl I liked. He accused me of trying to make a pass at his girlfriend and challenged me to a fight. He told his friends we were going to fight after school, and I was fearful all day. When the bell finally rang and I walked out of school, he was waiting for me, and a crowd had gathered to watch. We fought right in the block where I lived. He got the best of me in that fight, but after that, our relationship changed. I believe he gained a different respect for me, and we ultimately became friends. The girl we were fighting over paid no attention to either of us, but the event was the beginning of my growing self-esteem.

While all this was taking place, my mother was working more, and I wanted more from her than she was able to provide. I subsequently found myself attending church. On Sundays, I attended a church in my neighborhood; once again it was a place of safety and security. I gave my life to Christ and was baptized at an early age. I joined the choir, even though I couldn't sing; I was soon elected president of the youth choir. I made many new friends, and I looked forward to the fellowship at the church. The pastor took great interest in me, and he and his wife quickly became my spiritual parents. I spent many hours in their home; it was far different from ours, and I longed for their attention. Their son and I became best friends, and we grew closer and closer over the years. I went with them to other churches, where the pastor was invited to preach and became more active in the church. I loved to attend Sunday school and Baptist Training Union (BTU), and I met a strong man of God who became a powerful influence in my life. I will share more about his influence in my life in a later chapter.

As I reflect back, I realize God was putting strong men in my life who would provide me with the love and encouragement I needed. Sometimes we are unable to see blessings at the time they come, but we discover them later in life. Everything that happened in my younger years has contributed to who I am today. I have learned to be more appreciative of the things I have now, because of those lean days. I have learned the importance of a father loving his children as the result of the father I never had. I have even learned to be tender with my wife, because of the harshness I saw with my father. It is true; it's not where you start but where you finish that counts.

These first two chapters, my early childhood and my middle years, serve as a foundation of my early beginnings. Several more of these chapters will deal with some trauma in my life, and by the time you get to the end, you will see how every chapter speaks about the providence and hand of God on my life. These experiences speak to the heart of Romans 8:28—"And we know that God causes everything to work together for the good of those who love God and are called according to his purpose for them". There is very little good you have read or will read in the next few chapters, but keep on reading, and you will see for yourself the blessings of God. It is my prayer that you won't focus so much on my journey, but perhaps there is some similarity to your journey. Don't give up on your life and throw in the towel; God can turn it around. He can change all that has caused us pain into a blessing of gain. As someone said, "It is no secret to what God can do. What he has done for others, he can do for you too." Look at this book through the eyes of God.

Chapter 3

Challenging Years

A fter completing the ninth grade in junior high school, I started attending a vocational high school. I was totally confused at this time in my life about high school and what career I wanted to pursue. My counselors in junior high school suggested that the best school for me would be a vocational school. This was the result of some of my grades as well as my not really knowing what I wanted to do in life. At that time, many of the black students were selecting to attend vocational schools, with auto mechanics as their prime choice. I also selected auto mechanics, not knowing anything at all about the trade.

My first year was humiliating, to say the least. When I went to class, I was so embarrassed, for the harder I tried to follow instructions, the more difficult it became. From class we went to shop, where we had an opportunity to work on cars. I discovered early on that I wasn't mechanically inclined, and this was so evident, but I continued on and dreaded these classes. I was able to compete with the other classes, but auto mechanics was baffling. This is still evident today, for I have very little knowledge about repairing a car. I was successful graduating from tenth to eleventh grade, even though my grades in auto mechanics were poor. The eleventh grade really became a challenge.

While in vocational school, my activities at church increased and once again became the highlight of my life. It was a place of safety and security, and I neither had to compete in a classroom nor endure some of the pain at home. Church became like heaven on earth to me. I was accepted for who I was and even given leadership opportunities. I served as president of the junior choir and was very active in Sunday school and BTU. A deacon at church, whom I referred to earlier as a wonderful man of God, served as my mentor. He took such special interest in me, and I felt loved, just like I was his son.

I began to notice the girls, who were also paying attention to me, especially in church. They caused my self-esteem to increase as they flattered me with their words. I vividly remember how my sisters would have their girlfriends come to our home, and I always found a way to tell one particular girl how much I liked her. She really never paid me any mind, but that didn't stop me from giving her compliments. There were many girls at church, and I felt attached to all of them and enjoyed when they complimented me.

In the midst of all of this, studying became more challenging, and responsibilities at home continued to grow. My mother worked at a department store and even worked at times on the weekend doing housework for families. My grandmother, the matriarch of the family, was doing all she could to keep us together. Up until this time, we always rented our home until the landlord, who lived at the end of the block, got sick and passed away. The city sent us a notice that we would have to purchase the home or move. We didn't have the money to purchase our home, so I decided to quit school and go to work to help out.

I took a job as a bundle boy at a factory that made children's clothes. My job was to take bundles of clothes to various operators in an assembly line, one after another, until the coat was completely finished. This job was a new beginning in my life, and I found myself working and bringing my money home so our family would be able to buy our home. By the grace of God, we were able to purchase it. Working was something I really enjoyed, and I was beginning to feel confidence in myself. In the midst of all this, my grandmother died, and her loss really left a void in my life. Her death truly broke my heart, and I felt like a piece of me was also taken away.

I continued to work at the factory and remained involved in the church, and my social life increased on the weekends; I even found myself dating other girls. I enjoyed traveling with my church when they visited other churches; it seemed to mean so much to me at this time. I met a young lady at one of the churches we visited who was an usher, and that was the beginning of my love for her. We dated for a while, and I really thought this would be a long relationship. Then one day I went to visit her and was crushed when another guy was there when I arrived. I cannot put into words the disappointment I felt. It was another rejection for me.

I started to find other things to do to fill some of those empty places. I loved sports, and I began to be drawn to politics. I remember walking miles to a church in a snowstorm to hear a congressman as well as a pastor who spoke out for justice and equality for God's people. He was known to defy the political system and the media.

After working in the factory for a while, I joined the union and became part of Local 375, consisting of operators of various machines, bundle boys, janitors, and stock employees. There was no real advancement in these union jobs, but they provided benefits and job security. These jobs weren't high paying, but many of them were piecework jobs, and the operators of the machines were paid based on the work they were able to produce. I stayed at the factory for several years until a friend of mine was instrumental in helping me transfer to another more prestigious factory. There I assisted in the cutting room, where I separated the lining.

The cutters, who were the premier employees of the union, belonged to Local 110. They were mostly all-white males, and many of the workers who assisted them were African-Americans, in another Local 375. I found myself becoming more vocal in what I believed to be some unfair practices taking place in the union; I ran and was successful in becoming a delegate for my Local 375. I was sure to make my opinion known time and time again, much to no avail. I was often referred to as militant, because of my bush hairstyle, but I continued to make my voice heard in support of changes needed in our union and workplace. I never wavered in my convictions, even after being called a troublemaker.

While all this was taking place, I still felt some emptiness in my heart, even though I was dating several girls. They didn't fill the void I needed until I met a beautiful young lady, who captured my heart. She knew one of her friends had previously rejected me, but for some reason, I got the impression her girlfriend had said some nice things about me. She sparked my interest, and I pursued her with every ounce of energy I had. I found out she was dating someone else, but I was persistent, and we started to date. She was also involved in church and focused on her studies at a local university. Our lives were definitely on two different courses.

In the next chapter, you will see how God put two different people together to live a life of love.

Chapter 4
Changing Events in My Life

M any changes began to occur in my life. After much protesting and complaining, I was able to become a member of the more prestigious Local 110 and was still responsible for separating the lining materials for the garments, and I was determined to become a cutter, even though this local didn't have African-American cutters. There were several of us who ultimately became cutters, but you could count us on one hand. I regularly attended the union meetings and continued to raise concerns about the number of blacks employed as cutters throughout the city. I remember leaving the union meeting countless times, feeling hurt and frustrated that no one seemed to be listening, but I never wavered in my opposition to this racial bias. I was determined to bring about a change.

Life at home was still in chaos, and I found myself becoming more resentful toward my absent father, and my bitterness was very evident. As always, church was that constant place of fulfillment and security. I became more and more involved, and took on additional leadership responsibilities. On the weekends I would visit my girlfriend, Joan, who lived several blocks from our home. Her parents were divorced, and her stepfather was very stern. Her mother was cordial to me but made it plain and clear that her daughter was going to college and that she wasn't to have any serious relationships. She emphasized more than once, in her own way, that she wanted her to have the opportunity to meet someone also focused on college and a career. There were times when her words really pierced my heart, but I was still determined to date her daughter. She never referred to me as a high school dropout, as others had done; in fact, she encouraged me to pursue my dreams of being a cutter. Her words always provided me inspiration; therefore, I continued in my goal to be a cutter.

We had many things in common and truly enjoyed each other. She was also active in her church, and I admired that about her. My love for her really deepened, so I introduced her to my mother. I shall never forget what my mother said to me after meeting her. Her response pierced my heart. She had some reservations about her that I couldn't fully understand because she was so beautiful to me. I couldn't understand how anyone wasn't able to appreciate her; so once again, my relationship with my mother caused me to grieve. To think that my mother couldn't love her the way I did, with all that I had been through, was mind boggling. I never had the heart to share how my mother felt about her, so I'm not sure whether she ever knew. It is safe to say that they never really had a warm and fuzzy relationship though. I wanted to protect her from my mother's feelings, and that caused me to love her even more.

Our relationship became very serious, and I knew in my heart that in one way or another, she was going to be my wife. We loved going to the movies, visiting each other's church, and laughing together; we also loved to go dancing. She always had to be home at a certain time, and her parents wanted to know exactly where we were going and whom we were going with. They had no idea how much I really loved their daughter. She always provided me with so much inspiration, especially at the time when I received a call from a local union official informing me that I was going to be transferred to another factory and given a promotion. My heart leaped for joy, and the first thing I wanted to do was share this news with her. We rejoiced together, and this was the beginning of a new journey in my life.

I must admit that I was somewhat nervous but excited when I started working in this factory, especially since I had been labeled a troublemaker. I cannot even begin to count the number of times I did damage to garments as I was learning the trade. It was humbling, to say the least, but once again, she was my number one supporter and gave me the much-needed support and comfort I needed.

I remember one dark, dismal day in my life when my mother and I had a conversation about my dating and some other areas of my life that weren't pleasing to her. It seemed as though I could never do enough for her; she always had some harsh criticism. I became so distraught that I took some pills and tried to end my life. It was a horrible time for both of us. I remember her crying profusely because I had said some things to her I regretted and still regret to this day. Her words that night cut into the very core of my heart. I really didn't want to end my life; I had acted out of desperation. Somehow I was able to bring up those pills and spent the rest of the night crying myself to sleep.

Our relationship over the years improved, but we never got over some of those misunderstandings. I became defiant and determined that I was going to do things my way. I made a vow to myself that I wasn't going to let anyone rob me of my self-esteem. I really believe this was the defining moment of my life; not my mother, father, or anyone would tell me what I wasn't able to do. I began to develop secrets I held to myself to be sacred.

The parents of the love of my life were still keeping me at arm's length from her. Even though I had started dating their daughter more seriously, they continued to see me as a misfit. Seemingly there was nothing I could do to change their minds. They would say I was a nice young man but not good enough for their daughter. I told them about my promotion at the factory, but they didn't seem impressed. I shared with them my work in the church, and they simply acknowledged that that was good. I started to think about how she must have felt when she heard her parents talk about me, because she never gave me the impression that their thoughts of me influenced her. To the contrary, she always exhibited love and respect for me, and this true love caused me to propose to her. I didn't have the heart to ask her parents, because I knew what they would say.

I gave her an engagement ring on Christmas Day, but they made her give it back. My heart was crushed, and I made up my mind to confront them about their decision. They let me know very clearly that a ring wasn't acceptable; in fact, they went on to say that their daughter would never marry someone like me. They softened this by saying, "You can still come and visit her, but she will never marry you." I cannot tell you the hurt in my heart, but my love for their daughter was so deep that it caused me to accept what they had to say without anger; I was determined to prove them wrong.

We continued to date, and I made plans in my heart to marry this beautiful woman I loved very deeply. I also knew that for this to take place, I had to prove myself on this job. For every mistake I made, I endured the insults and criticism, and I continued to do the best I could to prove myself a cutter. I was blessed to become friends with one cutter who took a special interest in me, and he helped me to improve and learn from my mistakes. This allowed me to feel confident and able to increase my knowledge of this trade.

As I reflect back on these events, I realize more than ever that God was in the midst of all this. None of this took place by accident or chance; it was all in the providence of God. In every chapter, you will see the hand of God at work.

Chapter 5

My Marriage to Joan

L ove will cause you to do some extraordinary things. My love for Joan caused me to defy her parents and ask her to marry me. She agreed, and we made plans to get married without her parents knowing. I asked her mother whether we could visit my former pastor, who had relocated to another state; but before going there, we eloped and got married in Elkton, Maryland. For the first four months of our marriage, she lived in her home, and I lived in mine. No one knew about our marriage except the best man and his wife, who had traveled with us to Maryland.

During that time of living apart, we looked for and made an offer on a home. I wanted to purchase our first home, determined not to rent. When I applied for the mortgage, I didn't make enough money working at the factory, so I took a part-time job at a restaurant so I could meet the weekly salary requirement of the mortgage company and sustain the mortgage payments. This was really an exciting time for us; we would talk every day, holding those sacred moments in our hearts, keeping the secret from our family. As the days went by, I longed for the time for us to finally end our secret rendezvous.

I was so thrilled to hear from the mortgage company that our mortgage was approved. Every day we made plans of how we were going to tell her family we were married. At one point, she cried profusely, wondering what her parents would say. I then assured her we were going to continue as husband and wife no matter what came our way. Amazingly, we never got a chance to tell them because three days before going to settlement, her mother received a telephone call from the real estate agent, confirming our settlement date.

Needless to say, her mother was furious and angry, and those next few days were troubling, to say the least. Her mother lashed out at me with such anger, and her stepfather reacted in the same manner. Her mother threatened to have the marriage annulled and even accused her of being pregnant, but that was far from the case. She just couldn't believe we were purchasing a home, only because when they purchased their home, it had been many years later in their marriage. She threatened to come to church and tell the congregation what I had done, but as someone once said, "Time heals all wounds."

We went to settlement and immediately moved into our home with no furniture. A gentleman I met in church took us to a furniture store and cosigned for us to get a kitchen set, and that's all the furniture we had for a while. Her mother reluctantly allowed her to take her bedroom set, and she also gave us some dishes. Her mother and stepfather made a 180-degree turn and eventually became our strong supporters. On the other hand, my mother was still very distant to her and somewhat upset that she also hadn't been informed of our marriage.

We began to build our life together. Our first home was truly a blessing. From living from one part of the city to another, from steps to a porch, I felt like a king, and we were both so excited that God had blessed us with our first home. Little by little we began to purchase some furniture, and her mother was always bringing gifts to the house. She finally accepted the fact that I was her son-in-law, and our relationship began to grow. I was able to forget all the hurtful things she had said to me and found myself loving her, and she loved me. She was proud of her daughter in her early accomplishments: married with a home and a good career. My wife made many advancements in the medical profession at a local hospital, and her peers liked her. She was deeply involved in her medical career, so much so that every time someone in the family or I got sick, she would go to her medical book and look up the definition of the illness. We both attended church regularly, and I served as a trustee. I took on a part-time position as a waiter with a caterer on the weekend and gave up my job at the restaurant. Buying my first car was so exciting, and I remember to this day that I ran out of gas before I got it home. We had so many happy days together, even though I wasn't making a lot of money, but we pooled our money together and were able to meet our financial obligations. I loved surprising her with gifts on special days, holidays, and birthdays. We were young and daring, and she was everything a wife could be. Everywhere I went, I told others of this incredible woman God had blessed me to marry. She had a warm personality and a sense of humor, and we journeyed together in the sunlight of God's love. She continued to be my source of encouragement and was always ready with a listening ear and open heart to comfort me in the perfect times I needed it. As our relationship grew, there were still some concerns with members of our family. There were still some who couldn't rejoice over the blessings God had given to us.

We talked about starting a family, and I shared with her my dream to have a daughter. I already had a name chosen; it was Natalie. I really don't know to this day where the name came from; I just loved it. I have always loved girls, perhaps because of my relationship with my grandmother. In the next chapter, I will share with you the birth of our first child.

Chapter 6

Our First Child

We were excited about our first child being born. As I previously indicated, my weekends were devoted to working as a waiter for a caterer, doing many bar mitzvahs and weddings. While working one night, I served as a waiter for a young man named Todd, his name intrigued me. That name stayed with me and spoke to my heart. This young man had a wonderful personality and seemed to be so bright and articulate. Even though my heart's desire was for a girl, I thought that young man's name would be appropriate if I had a son. At the end of the evening I collected some cocktail napkins left on the table with his name on them, took them home, and placed them in our Bible.

Little did I know at the time that God would grant us in that year the birth of a son. As you may suspect, we gave him the name Todd, We were truly excited about our first son, and we received many expressions of love from our families and our church family. We were still struggling financially but were blessed with the generosity of the caterer I worked for who allowed us to have a wonderful reception following my son's dedication. We held it at a very exclusive catering facility, and we felt like a king and queen. I continued to work weekends and made every effort to attend church on Sunday mornings before I went to work.

I was blessed to be involved in leadership at church, but I somehow became troubled as the church transitioned to a new pastor. My insecurities caused me to feel uncomfortable. As I reflect back on those days, I cannot put my feelings on any one particular thing that caused me to feel uncomfortable. It was having my youthfulness and being defiant that caused me to struggle and no longer feel comfortable with my membership at this church. I was very engaged as a community activist and eager to get involved in the life of the community.

While working in the community, I became acquainted with a pastor's wife, and her commitment to the community moved me. The church she was a member of was quite large compared to mine, but again, the need to make a change was in my heart. I called and made an appointment to meet with the pastor on a Monday night. It was a wonderful meeting; I felt his warmth and sincerity, and I thought it was the perfect place where we could grow and develop. He made no effort to persuade me to change my membership; he just listened and advised me to be led by the Lord.

I went home that night and told my wife about the wonderful encounter I had with the pastor. I told her that I felt it was the place where the Lord could continue to speak to us and we could raise our son in the house of God. That next Sunday we went to the service and joined that day. It was the beginning of a wonderful relationship with that pastor and the church congregation. It felt like home, and the size of the church was of little or no concern because I felt wanted and affirmed. I was still seeking affirmation, and consequently it helped me overcome my insecurity and helped to develop me in some areas of leadership.

Before long our second son was born. In the same way that Todd's name inspired me, the name Marc and its spelling was a direct result of working at a catering event. I continued to keep the name Natalie in my heart, but we were again blessed with a son. We now had two sons and felt like we were living on top of the world. I was determined to try to be a good father and husband, for I'd missed that in my own youth. I was proud to be able to say I had two sons and carried their pictures with me and showed them proudly. My wife continued to work after the first and second pregnancies, and we were blessed to have a neighbor in the next block care for the boys during the day. We loved taking them to church on Sundays; it became one of the highlights of our week. She was a wonderful wife and loving mother, and our sons were her heart.

We were proud parents and thrilled to watch them grow and develop. I still insisted on having a daughter, even though our two sons added so much joy to our family. Each one had his own personality, yet each son was deeply loved. While they were growing, we continued to work and serve in our church. The boys were four years apart, and four years later, my wife was expecting our third son, Branden. You probably have already suspected where he got his name; yes, it was from another catering event. Here we were now with our sons, and at that point we realized a daughter wasn't in God's plans for us. We were happy and blessed as they added so many fulfillments to our lives. They each had features like their parents. We would recycle their clothes so they would have what they needed. We sought to treat them the same; in fact, for Christmas they would all get the same amount of gifts, with the same-size gift boxes.

I remember when the boys were young; I tried to take the wallpaper off our sons' room. I rented a machine that would scrape the paper off the wall and used a hose to run water from the bathroom which ran down into the dining room; it was a horrible sight. Needless to say, the house was a mess, and I finally had to hire someone to remove the wallpaper and paint the room. That was probably the first major conflict my wife and I had; she was really upset. Again, her love for me came to my rescue, and her anger turned into sympathy. Even though we were still struggling financially, we had some wonderful family time together. We had the family I always longed for and dinner together on Sunday after church. We were taking our sons to cultural activities and watching them grow, and they were saying in their own way how much they loved us. When we were unable to find a babysitter, my mother-in-law would step in and take care of them.

I remember Todd's first day of school and how he cried when we tried to leave. As many parents do, we took many pictures of that day. I lovingly became the parent to go to school and speak to the teachers about our kids' progress. I loved doing that with all my sons during their school years. We would attend parent/teacher night together, but for other times, I would be the one who went to school, particularly if a negative report was sent home. That seemed to happen quite a bit, yet we were blessed to see them move from grade to grade and make advancements in their studies and behavior.

All during our sons' younger years, I wrestled with my commitment to God. I was serving at church as president of the young adult fellowship. This was a wonderful ministry that bought young adults, married and single, together to engage in ministry, and we had a wonderful time of bonding and developed many friendships. This ministry provided me with another opportunity to cultivate my leadership skills. My thirst for God had deepened, and I felt there was something else God wanted me to do. I shared this with my wife, and she encouraged me to be open to God and talk to our pastor. At first I was reluctant to go any further, but at her insistence, I met with him and shared with him what I believed at that time was a call on my life to engage in Christian ministry.

Chapter 7
The Call to Christian Ministry

I remember meeting my pastor and sharing with him my call to the Christian ministry as if it had happened yesterday. I told him of the urgency I felt within my heart to preach. I also shared with him that the Lord had spoken to me some years earlier, but I had been reluctant. I felt that I was totally inadequate to proclaim the Lord's word, mainly because of my lack of education. My self-esteem was still very low, and I had so many insecurities.

It had been quite easy for me to push that feeling aside, but this time it was a feeling I couldn't resist. It was as if the Lord was knocking at the door of my heart and calling me by name to declare His name. While I shared with my pastor the inward feelings of my heart, I once again indicated some of my inadequacies. He listened very intensely and then said something to me I shall never forget: to go home, pray about it, and make sure I knew exactly what God was calling me to do. He didn't hesitate in encouraging me to take some time to consider all that was involved in what I called "the calling." He told me, "After you have given this consideration, meditation and prayer, then come back to me." His words were warm and affirming, yet I felt a sense of sternness. He prayed for me, and I left his office, moved by the power of God.

I went home and shared with my wife my conversation with our pastor. She asked me to think seriously about what I had asked him and told me she would support whatever decision I made. She wanted this to be my decision—not based on what she thought but rather on what God was leading me to do. For the first time in my life, I really took this matter of prayer seriously and sought God's guidance. It was indeed a soul-searching journey; so many thoughts came to my mind. I wrestled with God and myself, and felt the Spirit of God as I had never felt Him before.

About two weeks later, I called my pastor and asked whether I could meet with him. He didn't hesitate to set up a meeting and probably knew what I was going to say. At that meeting, I him told him I had no choice, since God had confirmed to me through prayer that this was something I must do. He shared pastoral wisdom with me; he simply said, as a father to a son, "You are a young man, and you need to get some education. You do not want your ministry to be marginal." He went on to speak to me about the need to complete my high school education and recommended that I take the necessary steps to complete my education. I was somewhat embarrassed that I lacked a simple high school education. It wasn't his words that caused me this embarrassment but my own lack of self-esteem. I didn't, however, let that fact deter me from taking his advice. I enrolled in a preparatory school and was able to complete my last year of high school in six months. I received my high school diploma and had a wonderful feeling of accomplishment.

Once again my pastor placed his confidence in me and encouraged me to move forward in the pursuit of higher education. He interceded on my behalf and spoke to someone at a Christian college regarding my enrollment. I was able to enroll there with little or no money but a strong desire to begin to develop some higher learning. I received some financial support from a ministry at church; that's about all I had at that time, but I really wanted to pursue a college education. My first semester was a true challenge. Walking on that beautiful campus gave me a feeling I cannot put into words. I was on cloud nine and pushed aside all thoughts of my struggles. I became a new person and was able to make many new friends. I loved to talk, and this was a way for me to break free from some of my inhibitions.

Going to college was an exciting time. I was in my early thirties with a wife and three sons, working a full-time job, and I was a college student. The college at that time had only a few African-American students. The population of students was mainly young, and there I was, walking on the campus with a bush hairstyle, which at that time symbolized being proud to be African American, and determined to take advantage of this wonderful opportunity God had given to me. I remember my first class; the professor outlined the syllabus, informing us of what the course required. My confidence waned a little, but once again I sought God in prayer.

I took a full-time load my first semester. I caught the train to school every day and made every effort to work hard and achieve this God-given goal. College life required much more than I anticipated. The tuition, the travel, the study, and the time I was away from home were at times overwhelming, but I continued to work hard, never wanting to quit. After the first semester, I decided to become a communications major, since this allowed me an opportunity to enhance my oral skills. Little did I know I would be required to take classes such as Shakespeare, theater, and drama. Just to stay ahead, I even took courses during the summer. My wife remained very supportive, even though this took a toll on our family. To stay on course, whenever the opportunity came, I also supplemented courses at a community college.

My busy life brought many, many challenges. I was the first in my family to attend college. College was just a dream, yet God allowed me the opportunity to begin to change the course of history for our family. While in college, I kept remembering being told numerous times that I would never amount to anything. Those words served as motivation to me. There were times when I felt like quitting, like when a professor returned a paper to me marked "unacceptable"; again, those negative words caused me to reach back into my inward self and write a new paper that became acceptable.

My involvement in a union would ultimately lead to a blessing. As I mentioned, I continued to work while going to school. I was missing some time, but up until this point, there were no significant consequences for doing so. Work was slow; therefore, it made it easier for me to miss time. As a union representative, I was involved in the negotiations for a new contract, and when the union and the company reached an impasse, our union went on strike, and we walked a picket line.

The situation between the union and my employer was very tense. A lot of negative words were said while on the picket line. I was one of the few African-American union members serving on the board during the strike; words were harsh and had some racial overtones. The strike lasted for about two weeks, and when it was finally settled, we went back to work. The owner of the company called me into the office and told me the union representatives had reprimanded him for speaking to me in the manner in which he did. He told me he hadn't been aware that I was a union representative, and at that point I made it clear he still had no right to speak to me the way he did, with little or no respect. Surprisingly, he apologized.

I know God was working in this situation and changing my life, for I remember a time when I wouldn't have accepted this apology and would have acted ungodly. I humbled myself and accepted his apology, for I felt he really meant what he said. I was grateful for the opportunity just to have employment given all I was dealing with as a full-time student. I took this opportunity to share with the owner my enrollment in school and asked whether I could work part time to continue my education. He asked me what I was going to school for and why at this point in my life, and I shared with him my call to the ministry. He commended me on what I was accomplishing and agreed that I could continue to work part time. This agreement allowed me not only to work part time but also to work on Saturdays for overtime. The company's policy required me to work forty hours prior to any part-time pay, but he allowed me to work on Saturdays, even though I didn't meet that requirement. He was very helpful and supportive in my educational pursuit. I know that was nothing but God opening up the door.

For several years I was able to work, go to school, and keep my union benefits. What was originally a disaster turned into a blessing. I couldn't have gone to school without his support. I shall never forget that encounter and his willingness to help me move forward in life. All the while, things were getting worse financially at home. Our gas was turned off, and we found ourselves with bills mounting, yet my wife remained very supportive. She even went to our pastor and asked him whether I knew what I was doing. She told him she was at wits' end and didn't know how we were going to continue to provide for our family. He assured her that God was going to make a way. Never once did he waver in his support for me and our entire family. He became an encourager to her and would often call and check on her, just as he checked on me.

I know now that I put my family through a lot. Sometimes, even to this day, there are those who call me stubborn. That may be true in some cases, but I rather think of my having tenacity and endurance, because without them I couldn't write this chapter or this book. I had no other choice than to stay the course, even though there were so many setbacks along the way.

I started driving back and forth to school; then one night my car broke down, and I was stranded for hours with no way to get home. One of my classmates passed by, saw me in distress, and took me home. I remember giving God thanks for someone coming to my aid. The car was old and needed a lot of repairs, and because I had no money, I couldn't have it repaired. I then started catching the train to school and got home quite late at night, which left little time for family or study. My grades were never great, but they weren't bad. Finances, family, and study were a struggle for me, but I was determined to finish what I had started. I was at a point where my grants and loans ran out of resources.

One day during my last year in school, I was called into the dean's office and told I would no longer be able to remain at the college, because there was no funding available. That was a heartbreaking conversation. I sat in the dean's office with tears running down my cheek; I had really run out of resources. I felt so alone, and there was a terrible feeling that came over me. Here I was, so close to the finish line and being told I could no longer continue my studies. It was like a death sentence. Can you imagine never dreaming to go to college, going there, and then being told you can't finish.

I dropped my head and was speechless. All I'd learned about communication was to no avail; there was nothing I could say or do. I made my way home and told my wife my dream had ended. We prayed together, and I wept in pain. A few days later, I received a call from the dean's office and was informed that someone had heard about my plight and paid my last year of tuition. I asked who this person was and was told he or she wanted to remain anonymous. I kept asking about this person and was told he was of another color, a man of deep faith who loved God's people. This person provided many generous gifts to the college and its students.

Once again God had come to my rescue. This generous person paid my entire last year of tuition, and because of his generosity and the gifts of many others, I graduated from college with a bachelor of arts in communications. It was one of the greatest days of my life. My wife, mother, and sons were there right by my side. I shall never forget walking across that stage and receiving my diploma. It was well worth all the sacrifice and tears. I never thought in my wildest dreams that I would ever see that day come, but God's goodness and mercy allowed me to be part of that graduating class.

The call to ministry resulted in my reaching another milestone in life. God was moving, and I was continually being blessed. On December 1, 1974, I preached my initial sermon titled "Thinking Time." I shared how Paul, on his way to Damascus, was knocked off his beast, and the Lord gave him "thinking time." That experience changed his whole life, from Saul to Paul. My thinking time changed my entire life. I still remember that night; when I finished preaching, I had so many eight-and-a-half-by-eleven sheets of paper, and I must have preached every word on those papers. I heard people comment, "He's a fine young man." I still chuckle that I didn't hear any compliments about the sermon, rather they did offer compliments about my Christian character. today. Even after my initial sermon, my pastor never wavered in his devotion to me.

Chapter 8

Ministry Unfolding

U pon my graduation from college, I enrolled as a part-time student in seminary. This was another exciting time in my life as I began to really study the Word of God; ministry was unfolding, and I was rejoicing. My pastor, Reverend Dr. Albert Franklin Campbell provided me with several opportunities to preach. I was the worship leader and had many preaching engagements as the result of my pastor's leadership. Several years later, he recommended me for ordination, which took place in October 1977. I was a licentiate at our church, and Pastor Campbell gave me several opportunities to preach the gospel of Jesus Christ. I was also invited to preach at several churches and was grateful for those opportunities.

By the grace of God, I was called to my first church. Pastor reminded me there is a church for every pastor, and this congregation would be a great opportunity for me to begin my pastorate. He indicated that pastoring at this church could be a blessing for them as well as for me; he was absolutely right. My experiences there were remarkable. It was a small congregation, with members full of love and devotion. They blessed me in so many ways; I shall always be indebted to them for the opportunity to be their shepherd for seven years. They suffered with me as I preached from those long manuscripts. The congregation was open to receiving me as their pastor, with my wife being the first lady and my sons being part of the church family. They weren't able to provide me with a large salary and medical benefits, but they gave me much more in love offerings, sacrificial gifts, and just a willingness to serve God. It was a huge undertaking, but we were blessed to make some necessary renovations to the sanctuary, which needed a lot of repairs.

I vividly remember when my car needed repairs; it was an old car, but it was a blessing for me to have it. One of the deacons spent hours—and I do mean hours—repairing it, and the church paid for all the repairs. That was just one act of the many expressions of love shown to me and my family.

The congregation was kind to me in every phase and facet of my life, especially enduring my long sermons. I thought of my pastor's remarks. "We learn to preach by preaching." I was really learning, but no one ever criticized my preaching or told me I was too long other than my wife. She was my biggest support and critic. We often joked about my preaching and pastoring, but she was always full of encouragement. These were happy days, and the congregation was willing to follow me as I followed God. I really don't remember any bad experiences with the congregation; they were happy, and I was happy, and hopefully God was pleased. I remember doing our church's first radio broadcast, which was on at midnight. I would go to the radio station once a week at midnight and bring a Word from the Lord. This was my first experience with radio, and being a communications major was very helpful.

My sons sang in the choir and were active in church; we were like the ideal Christian family, going to church on Sunday and looking forward to coming home after the service to one of my wife's fine meals. There were dinners after worship services on many Sundays, so on those days, we enjoyed dinner at church. We watched our sons grow and develop into fine young Christian youth. Things seemed to be going so well; I couldn't imagine anything that spelled trouble down the road. My oldest son graduated from high school and was in college, making us proud parents.

Just when we were at this high point in our lives, things started to fall apart. My wife began complaining of back pains, and this pain became so severe that after visiting with her doctor, he recommended that she schedule a biopsy. She underwent the procedure; it was one of the darkest days of my life. Immediately after the procedure, the doctor came out and told me he had some bad news. She had lung cancer, and her life-span was less than six months. I couldn't believe what he was saying; I was knocked off my feet and remember shaking like a leaf, trying to digest what I had just heard and thinking about what I could do about it.

She'd smoked for many years and quite a bit. The doctor informed me that lung cancer was one of the worst kinds of cancers. I tried to find a way to brace myself to see her after I had just heard the news. I thought I could conceal it, but tears ran down my face like rivers of water. She too was crying, and we were speechless for a while; then I held her hand and said, "We are going to make it through this by the grace of God." After we prayed, I asked the doctor about the plan of treatment he was suggesting. He recommended chemotherapy with efforts to reduce the tumor and ease her pain, but again he didn't provide any real hope.

For the next few days, we pondered how we would tell our sons. Our oldest was away at college, and we really wanted him to finish, so we were reluctant to share this news with him. We didn't tell our other sons about the severity of their mom's illness, just that their mother was sick. We continued to put on a good front, attending church and trying to live normal lives, but each day her body was weakening. Her chemotherapy treatments started, and it took a toll on her appetite; she lost a considerable amount of weight.

I informed the church of her condition; they were very supportive. I couldn't have made it without them. Our youngest sons would come home from school every day and see their mother in bed or moving slowly around the house. As she got weaker, I had to cook our meals; that was an experience in itself. We ate a lot of frozen dinners and my specialty, "magnificent tuna." I really couldn't cook; I couldn't fry chicken, but I did well with pork chops, and we managed to eat. This was a time when we truly bonded together as a family. All the while, her body began to decay.

There was one lady, who has now gone on to glory, who would come to the house every day to give my wife her medication and often bring us dinner, which gave me the relief she knew I needed. There were several hospital stays, and finally the day came when she was bedridden. I would be up during the night as she cried out in agony, and I'm sure my sons heard their mother crying in the midnight hour. Even today, I still struggle to make hospital calls, particularly to persons who have cancer or some other critical condition. I watched this beautiful woman God had given to me be reduced to pain; the agony was much more than I could bear.

We engaged hospice, and they were extremely helpful in providing care and support not only to me but also to my sons. I have a great deal of respect for those who serve in this vital care component for people. She was once again admitted to the hospital, and this time she didn't come back home. I wanted my sons to remember their mother with all her beauty, so I didn't take them to the hospital to visit her, and I went alone many times. Finally, I received a call in the middle of the night that God had called her home. She was only thirty-nine years old.

The next morning I had to tell the boys their mother had passed away; that task was very hard. I then had to call our oldest son at college. He'd left home to go to college with his mother in her youthfulness and beauty, only to hear the news that she was no longer alive. What does one say about God and His love when He takes away someone who is young and full of life? I'm still not sure what to say, but I know God is a comforter and provider. I had made so many funeral arrangements for other families; now this time I had to make my own. My pastor was there with us the entire time, so I called on him to share in her home-going service.

The service was held on a Sunday evening, and the church was packed. Many of my friends I hadn't seen in a while were there as well as many of her friends. It was a cold December evening, and I could feel the cold wind blowing. Pastor preached a beautiful eulogy, and the choir sang anthems. It was a service well fitting for this woman of God. The next day we went to the cemetery, and I stood there with my sons, heavy of heart and thinking of the beginning of a new life. I didn't know what lay ahead without my wife and a mother for the boys, but somehow, as the wind blew in the cemetery that day, I felt God was going to provide.

Christmas was just a few weeks away. I knew she would have wanted the boys to have a special Christmas, but I didn't know how it was going to happen. She had insurance, and I was able to use it to pay for her funeral; the few dollars left I used to make Christmas meaningful for my sons. We had a Christmas tree and gifts, but there was still a void I couldn't fill.

Chapter 9

The First Winter

As the holiday season passed and the cold days of January arrived, I felt the darkness of the winter inside our home. Our oldest son went back to school, heavy of heart. The younger boys were under my total care; I didn't have a wife I could cling to, and they didn't have a mother to embrace them. There was sadness in our home; darkness seemed to come so early. There were many times I longed for the breaking of a new day. I helped them with their homework, made visits to their school, and provided them with a good dinner each evening. I often thought of the words she'd said to me as she was in her last days with tears in her eyes. *I'm glad it's me God is calling home, because I couldn't take care of the boys the way I know you can.*

She'd had so much confidence in me. I knew I could never take her place, because her love for our sons was beyond description. I couldn't even pack their lunch the way she did. She had a knack of making everything so special. As I mentioned earlier, I was a terrible cook, and we ate so many frozen dinners. Every time we got an offer from someone at church to bring us a meal, I accepted graciously. I thank God the church was there, providing wonderful meals for us. Winter seemed to be so long; I couldn't wait for the spring; trying to pastor, work, and provide care for my sons was a tremendous challenge. I got a little relief when I was laid off from work, thus freeing up some of my time. I was thankful I could collect unemployment to help supplement my salary from the church. There were so many challenges. I made a decision to discontinue my studies in seminary and devoted my time to my family and my church.

My sons were such a blessing; we bonded together in such a rich and meaningful way. I was able to reflect on how God gave me the opportunity to be a father to my sons, as I had always prayed for. I didn't want them to experience what I had experienced from my father. What I didn't know was how God was going to prepare me for this role as father. I had no choice; God had taken their mother home, and I had to be there for them, exactly what I had prayed for.

We had some wonderful times together. There were times when I thought I was encouraging *them*, but the reality was, they were encouraging *me*. They never complained about my poor cooking or my sometimes-overbearing concerns as a father. I wrote my oldest son in college regularly, but I couldn't tell how he felt in his heart. I suspected he might have been angry at God, at me, or even at the fact that his mother hadn't told him about her cancer. But it was our desire that he, being our first, would continue and finish college. The youngest boys shared the same room together, so they were a comfort for each other. That comfort wasn't there for him, and, sad to say, there was a time when I wasn't there for him.

Through this whole experience, I learned so many things about myself, God, and the challenges of life. I still refer to that time as a "frame of reference," for the passing of my son's mother was the lowest point in my life, yet I knew that if God could bring me through that, He could bring me through anything.

My sons had chores to do around the house, and they did them without too much complaining. Spring finally came and brought a true ray of sunshine. The days were longer, the sun seemed to be brighter, and some healing took place. We looked forward to Easter and the real beauty of spring. My oldest son came home for spring break, and we all had an opportunity to spend some quality time together. He was still very reserved, and they all seemed to be healing and being boys at that age. I remember going to school on parents' night and having to speak to them about their behavior. I would have them sit on the sofa and give them a long sermon, which I still think they paid little or no attention to, but they knew a sermon was coming.

We went to church together, and at times I felt as though some of the love the congregation had for us had turned to pity. That isn't what we wanted, so the boys became a little more reserved about how they would speak and act when it came to their mother. Spring also gave us an opportunity to share my favorite pastime, baseball, and I took them to several games. None of the boys were true baseball fans, but they went with their dad to keep me happy. Their real love was basketball, which they played regularly. I tried to do as much housecleaning as possible, but I must admit it was nothing like my wife would do.

Even though spring offered some relief, there were still voids in all our lives. We learned about avoidance; that is to say, we just didn't talk about it. I knew if I dwelt too much on her death, I would be no good to myself or to my sons. It is amazing how things stay with you. The hospice social worker told me I needed to be able to care for myself, because my sons couldn't lose two parents at the same time. There were times when I just put on a front, but deep down inside I was hurting. I was able to grasp the beauty of the words in Psalm 30:5, "Weeping may last through the night, but joy comes with the morning". My sons gave me so much joy, and the gospel gave me so much hope. I really longed for my wife, but I knew having her back wasn't possible.

As spring drew near to a close and the loneliness remained, I thought about what it would feel like to go out on a date. I never really wanted to bring any woman into our home. I had been told on many occasions about the need for a period of time or what people would say in terms of being appropriate, but I also knew what my wife had given me and what I needed. There were several persons at church who seemed to be waiting for me to say something to them, because I felt the gestures they were making and didn't want to lead anyone on. I was looking perhaps not so much for a date but for someone to have a conversation with, yet I didn't want to have that relationship impact my pastorate. In the next chapter, I will share how one of those friends became more than a friend.

Chapter 10

The Beginning of a New Relationship

A s I thought about beginning to have a conversation with a woman of God, I spent some time with God, reflecting on the many meaningful moments that had taken place during my wife's illness. As I mentioned previously, we received a lot of support from family and friends. Tanya, one of my wife's friends, who was very warm and caring and served with her in a ministry at our church, came to visit with us and brought meals. I thought she would be someone I might want to have a conversation with.

I remember her calling our home and inquiring about how things were going with us. Her voice was pleasant with a sound of genuine concern. I called her, and we began with small talk; I just needed someone to talk to. There was nothing heavy in our initial conversations, but it was a form of relief I began to look forward to. The calls increased throughout the week, and sometimes calls were made late at night when my sons were asleep. I finally asked her whether we could meet for coffee.

That first meeting turned into many. What started off as a conversation about God and family turned toward each other's journey. She told me she was dating someone and was involved in a pretty serious relationship. On the other hand, I was just looking for company and companionship. From our first time around coffee, the meeting soon became dinner. I really enjoyed her company; she was beautiful and intelligent, and she had a heart for God. As I shared with her my experiences, many she was aware of, she shared with me the pain in her life from losing a young daughter in a fire. She had one son, Darrell. He became my fourth son, and I have watched him become a strong man of God. Little did I know that God was about to bring healing to both of our lives. I never intended for this to be a love relationship, but God knew what I needed. I believe with all my heart, even now, that God had already planned that our two hearts would become one.

She was a very independent and successful woman working in corporate America, and she had been through a divorce. She was very secure about who she was and what she wanted to do with her life. On the other hand, here I was, with three sons and a very limited income. I didn't have a lot to offer but a caring heart. She made it very clear from the very beginning that she wasn't looking for a husband and certainly not one with baggage. She repeated to me more than once that she was already in a relationship and had no desire to end it. But I just kept talking, and the more I talked to her, the more I realized the quality in her life. My younger sons knew of her, since she had come to our home on many occasions, but they really didn't know of the feelings developing in my heart for her.

I tried to suppress these feelings at times because I didn't want to get hurt, particularly when she indicated all we could be were friends. The more I saw of her, the more she touched my heart. There were feelings I couldn't control, and I knew she was someone I could really love. The more I tried to convince her that our meeting wasn't accidental, but rather the providence of God, the more she held firm that she was comfortable where she was. We continued to spend time together; and then there were times when I sent her a card or simply placed some candy on her doorstep.

I finally got enough nerve to tell my sons I was going to dinner with her. Those dinners increased, and so did my love for her. What started out as a friendship turned into a pursuit. The person God made me, in terms of taking risks, having tenacity, and being bold all came together. The more she said no to my advances to increase our relationship, the more I said yes to my desire to win her for myself. It was exciting to pursue this beautiful, gifted, caring woman. Her resistance gave me persistence. She did indicate to me that she wasn't open to raising children, giving the pain she'd experienced with the death of her child; I took the initiative to ask her to pray with me regarding our journey, and we sought God for direction. My sons were at the top of my heart, and I wanted to fill some of the voids in their lives as the result of not having a mother. I knew the great void in my own life and also recognized that theirs was just as heavy.

They seemed to like Tanya at first, but again, for them she was just someone who had been there during their mother's illness. At that time, they didn't see her as a mother figure. I did, and I also saw her as one who could share with me the journey of life. Besides the apprehensions she had about being a wife and mother, another was of me, the preacher. She was well involved in ministry at church, where she had been a member for many years, but the thought of leaving her church and becoming "first lady" of my church, a church she hardly knew anything about, and one that was certainly different from her church in many ways, was difficult. We discussed her being first lady, my finances, even my being pastor. All I had to offer was myself and what God was able to do in spite of my current situation. So I continued to try to woo her with every ounce of energy in me.

One night I took her to dinner and gave her an engagement ring. We hadn't been seeing each other that long, but my mind was made up, and I knew this was what I wanted; I was going to do everything possible to make it happen. She took the ring but quickly gave it back. She reminded me that the relationship she'd told me about earlier was still very much part of her. I acted as though I didn't hear her and felt there was a bond between us that God had given that was stronger than she or I could break. I knew she loved me in spite of her resistance, for there was no way she would have continued with what she thought to be just a friendship when she knew I thought it to be something more. There are many things I remember, such as how she spent hours on the phone with me; I recall her gentle smile and warm embrace, her telling me of of her prayers and what she really wanted out of life, and her describing how she wanted one day to have a family and to be more involved in church. I knew she couldn't deny her feelings, and I wasn't about to relinquish the gift I knew God had given me in her.

The struggle of whether she should accept the ring or let me go another away was real. I also knew there were those who were talking about my affection for her because it was so obvious to those who knew me. They said, "It's too soon," "He's still grieving," or "He doesn't know what he is doing." Once again I never lost sight of my need to have her in my life.

I shared with my sons that I had proposed to her. They didn't know she had returned the ring, but I wanted them to know from their father what I had done, all the while still thinking to myself that she would ultimately accept the ring. The ring was a symbol of my heart; even though I had it back, she had my heart. I knew it was easier for her to give back the ring than to give her heart. I relied on her heart to bring us together, and by the grace of God, her heart stayed with me, and she said yes to my proposal.

Chapter 11

The Wedding Date

A fter much prayer, I spoke to my pastor regarding my intentions to get married. He didn't seem surprised but offered his prayers and support for us. Once again I felt his genuine concern for my well-being, and he provided me with some pastoral counseling for the new journey I was about to begin. Not only did I have a great admiration for my pastor, but I was truly inspired by his devotion as a husband to his wife and a father to his two sons. I cherished what he stood for as a family man and appreciated the way he spoke in glowing words about his marriage. Once again he fulfilled some of the voids in my life regarding a father figure. After receiving his blessings for our marriage, I knew this was the providence of God.

I informed my church of my intentions; there were mixed emotions, but some expressed joy others remained silent. We began to make plans for our wedding, and the excitement of this new love continued to build. The days went by swiftly, and there was a yearning in my heart for the day to finally come. We had a wonderful wedding and reception at my pastor's church, and we began an unbelievable journey. That day I was full of anxiety, and the events of the day caused me to break out in hives. We went on our honeymoon, and I'm sure there were times that week when she felt peculiar, for it was far from a honeymoon; I was absorbed with thinking of our sons and still getting flashbacks of my wife's death. She sensed some unrest in my spirit but gave me space to work through my emotions.

We decided we wanted to begin anew. I sold my home, she rented out her home, and we bought our first home together. My income at this time was very low; therefore, she supported much in the way of our finances. She never complained and shared generously with our sons, making our home a wonderful place for our family. We now enjoyed delicious meals as well as warmth and love in our home, which had been missing. Of course, our sons thoroughly enjoyed her cooking. She was very meticulous about keeping our home neat. We truly began to bond as a family. As a blended family, we experienced some challenges, but both of us had a growing desire to make our marriage meaningful and fruitful.

She became involved as first lady of our church, and the members received her with warm and caring hearts and hands. She continued to be a source of encouragement to my ministry, and we were inseparable at times. I learned so much about myself in the early years of our marriage, and I learned more about God. There were ups and downs, highs and lows, but like all couples, we knew they were simply part of two lives coming together. God gave me this beautiful, gifted woman of God as my wife and a second chance for love. I was astonished that God had granted me joy and fulfillment in the midst of pain and sorrow. It is said that beauty lies in the eye of the beholder; when I behold her in my mind, I see all her beauty and a warm, caring, and compassionate woman. Sometimes she can be fiery but always passionate. God has granted me this rich blessing to have her as a wife, mother, and friend. Even today I marvel that God is able to restore lives that have been torn apart. He did that for me, and I am forever grateful that we share in parenting and doing ministry together.

She began to feel the restlessness in my heart regarding my pastorate at our church. I wanted so much for the people to grow. I loved them, and I knew they loved me, but something was still missing. They were a caring people, and I felt the need to serve them with all my heart, soul, and mind. I felt the church couldn't really grow in its present location, but I didn't want to lead them to another site without a strong commitment to remain with them. I felt God tugging at my soul. I preached as a candidate at several congregations, but nothing happened. I'm not sure whether they knew I was candidating; if they did, they never let me know.

We prayed about where the Lord would lead us, though it was disappointing at times to be a candidate and not be called, but once again she was there for encouragement. While encouraging me, she also provided support for our sons. Todd, was in college, and we would drive to pick him up, and she would make sure he had all the things a college student needed. The younger boys were growing up and continuing their studies in school. She provided love and discipline at the same time, and that was challenging at times. We continued to pray for God to intervene in the lives of all our sons.

I remember one Christmas Eve when I received a call from a church in the Northeast, indicating that they were going to place my name before the congregation as pastor. I was excited, but I told her I wished it was the church where I had preached on several occasions. Well, once again, God did something amazing. Several hours later that day, I received a call from that church, indicating their desire to place my name in as pastor. I couldn't believe what had taken place in those several hours. She was a little cautious because she knew I had been let down before; her concern for me has always been the hallmark of her love. I believe with all my heart that that's what makes her so special. She is much more reserved than I and more cautious, and I often act impulsively; but again we complement each other. God was about to bring forth a new blessing in our lives, and the new church would be that blessing.

Chapter 12

The Call to Bethlehem

I vividly remember a conversation I had with Deacon Philip Smith at Bethlehem Baptist Church. He indicated to me that I was the candidate the church decided to vote on. My heart beat rapidly, and I was indeed grateful that God had heard my prayers. Deacon Smith shared with me that my name would be placed before the Bethlehem congregation in March of the coming year. I felt the need to be honest with him so he would know I was a candidate for the Hill Congregation. I didn't want to take anything for granted, knowing how I had been so close before only to find myself disappointed. Without naming the church, I indicated to Deacon Smith the Hill church was going to vote in January, and I felt that if they were to call me as pastor, I would accept the call. My heart was with Bethlehem though, where I had preached on several occasions and met many members of the congregation as well as the leadership; and I was really excited.

Deacon Smith was a very caring man of God, and he truly knew my heart. He said to me, "Let me get back to you as we may be able to move our vote to an earlier date." He then shared with me the voting process and said that they needed a three-fourths majority of the members present to elect a pastor. They decided I would be their only candidate, and if I were successful in that voting process, I would be their new pastor.

That Christmas Eve and Christmas Day are ones I shall never forget. I shared the news with our sons, and they were excited, which lifted my soul. I began to pray and ask God whether He would give me the desires of my heart. I called my pastor and shared with him the events that had taken place over the last several days. He prayed with me once again that all would be well. A few weeks later, Deacon Smith called to inform me that he was able to move the church vote up to January, still abiding by the requirements of the constitution, which mandated the three-fourths majority vote.

Believe me, the day they voted was an anxious day in January. I later learned what occurred that evening; it was nothing but the providence of God at work. The senior pastor of another church chaired the meeting. It is my understanding that he put the vote on the floor, and I missed being called as the pastor by one vote. The objections of my being called were based on the fact that I had remarried after my wife's death. There were those who interpreted my remarrying to be against God's will. The chairman of the meeting, whom I had come to know and admire, spoke out on my behalf. He assured the congregation that my remarrying wasn't in violation of God's will. He informed them that God had called my wife home to glory, and since I was a father and one he knew to be a caring individual, he persuaded the congregation not to allow that to get in the way of calling me. He spoke from his heart at length about what he knew about me. He believed me to have great character and total commitment as a husband and father.

As a result of his passion, he was able to call for another vote. I was voted as pastor-elect with one vote over the requirement needed. The chairperson called me that night and began the conversation with "Brother pastor"—that was his affectionate way of speaking to or about me— "you have been elected as our pastor." I let out a shout and began to give God praise and thanks for the new opportunity He'd granted to me. God had given me is favor and I expressed my gratitude by thanking Him over and over again."

I knew I had to inform the members of my current congregation that I was about to accept the pastorate at another church. I believed there were some members who would be upset, as they had grown to love me and I had come to love them. I assured them that my love for the church was deep, but I felt God was calling me to assume responsibility at a place the Lord had prepared for me. We prayed together, and I asked them whether they would grant me the opportunity to share my journey with the church so they would hear from me.

I called a meeting with the deacons and trustees to inform them of my decision. They were prayerful, complimentary, and supportive. I then spoke to the congregation to inform them I would be leaving in the next two months. There were tears, well-wishes, prayers, and an abundance of love I felt from the heart of God's people. They were my first love, and it was hard for me as well to bid them farewell. As I indicated earlier in this book, they were such a blessing to me, and I shall always remain grateful to God for that congregation.

The next two months of transition were filled with mixed emotions. The members gave our family a wonderful send-off with prayers, gifts, and a beautiful reception. I still have some of the cards the members wrote, expressing their love for me.

Chapter 13

My First Days at Bethlehem

My last two months seemed like eternity, and I couldn't wait until the day came when I would be pastor-elect at the new church. During those two months, I would often ride out to the church, sit in the parking lot, and gaze at the building. The excitement ran deep in my heart. The day finally came, and I preached my first sermon to the people of God. The church was full, and my family and I were well received. There was no reference to me as pastor-elect; they simply greeted me as pastor. We had one service at eleven o'clock in the morning, and it was truly a blessing. The choir sang hymns of praise, and prayers were offered on behalf of me and my family. A true exciting moment was being presented with the keys to the church. Many persons came from the small-knitted community as well as persons who weren't members of the congregation.

During the first several weeks, the chairperson took me around to the homes of members in the community. We would walk the streets and go in and out of homes; it was a blessing I will always remember. This community was very close; everyone knew each other, and many talked at great lengths about the history of the church. Not being from that area, they would speak of it as if it was miles away. The first encounter I had with the death of one of the members was something I recognized and was part of their expectations. God had called one of the members home, and the family wanted me to come to their house and pray over the deceased person before the body was removed. I soon realized this expectation was ingrained in the lives of the community. I was able to accommodate them, but I must admit that it was something I wasn't accustomed to, and I soon realized there were many other expectations too. In many of their minds, it was *their* church, and they would often remind me of the nineteen founders, of how the families built the church, and of their deep commitment to the church. Being new to the community, I didn't respond; I just listened. Their pride for their church was deep, and their love for the Lord was apparent. They were community minded, and I soon became part of their community.

The honeymoon between pastor and people was in high gear, and I came to love and respect them, and with whatever was said, I didn't react to it but simply listened. They were all very proud of their church with the very nice, beautiful sanctuary tucked away in a quiet community just outside the city. I soon learned some of the history of the church, which recorded it as being bombed during the civil rights struggle. They had other challenges, but the people were faithful and very proud of their accomplishments.

We had a traditional African-American service at the eleven o'clock hour, and most of the members walked to church. The community was predominantly African-American, many of whom had migrated from another state and settled there, working in a variety of businesses. Many were schoolteachers, county workers, laborers, and people from all walks of life, working together and seeking to build strong families. Many members of the congregation had been there for forty to fifty years, and their families had been members before they were. The organist was the very heart of the ministry of music. She loved the church, played the organ, and led the choir with a heart that expressed love to God.

I received a wonderful reception to the church—not only from the members but also from members of the community. We began to plan for my installation service. My first pastor, Rev. Edward I. Satchel, pastor of the New Mt. Zion Baptist Church in New York, was the preacher. I was truly grateful that he could share in this significant day in the life of our new congregation. I would never have thought in my wildest dreams, after growing up under his leadership that I would now be pastoring. The church that had licensed and ordained me played a significant part in that day and the days that followed. My pastor, Rev. Dr. Albert F. Campbell, pastor of Mt. Carmel Baptist Church, along with his congregation, came out in large numbers for the afternoon installation celebration. The choir, under the direction of their organist for more than sixty years, filled the choir loft. Some of the choir members had to sit in the congregation because the choir loft was full. Chairs were put in the aisles for worshippers, and some even had to stand. Local community leaders and politicians were also present.

This was the first installation service for us, and my wife looked so beautiful that day. Our sons surrounded us, and my mother was also present. Pastor Campbell preached a powerful sermon and spoke about a marriage between pastor and people, and my heart was lifted as he spoke of me as his son. There was a wonderful reception following the service, and we were showered with prayers, gifts, and cards. This day of jubilation was full of God's blessings. I have pictures in my office today to remind me of that day, one I shall never forget as long as I live.

Chapter 14

Growing Pains

T he installation service was over, and I was no more pastor-elect but
pastor, and I realized, as never before, a tremendous challenge. The
excitement was over, and now it was time to assess the life of our
congregation. In my own excitement we developed the theme of "The
most exciting church in the suburbs." I wanted the congregation to
embrace my excitement, and they did. Many members anxiously waited
to embrace some new innovative ways of doing church. I continued to
move throughout the community to spread the word about our church;
we even distributed flyers and posters in the community.

One of my first ventures was to put together our first church
directory, which my pastor so effectively used for many years. This
church directory would include the names of all persons who served in
leadership, the meeting dates and time of ministries, and the calendar
of events for the entire year. We continue to use the church directory
today, updating it every year. There was one staff person in the office.
I became attached to her, and she became a very strong encourager and
supporter. One of my first challenges was to seek to get her a five-dollar
increase. She wasn't a member of the church, but her husband served
as one of our trustees; I was unable to get that done. That might have
been my first setback, but surely it wouldn't be my last.

The deacons were the pillar of the church along with the trustees;
they literally governed the church, and I had to learn how to work

| 53 |

with them. I was under the impression that they really wanted change, so I constantly looked at new ways of doing ministry. I knew change was hard, but I was determined to work together to bring about the necessary changes for the church to grow. This community church had a strong history I was deeply appreciative of, but I also knew we would have to make some changes to grow, and I truly thought that was why they had called me as pastor. I knew the change would take some time, but I also knew God had called me to this church to expand our ministry. To many, a pastor only preached on Sunday and allowed the officers to run the church.

There were some wonderful people in the congregation when I arrived, but many of them were set in their ways. I had come to love them, and I believe they were beginning to love me. I was grateful that God had given me the opportunity to serve them, and I was committed to serve them with every ounce of energy within me. I received so much encouragement from the congregation, as well as from the deacon chairman, who always sought to lift me up in prayer and support me as a man of God. His love for his church and his pastor was evident.

In my early days at the church, plans were under way for the centennial celebration, which would be in a few years. I was called in 1986, and the centennial would be in 1988. Their initial planning was to celebrate the day without a preacher yet recognize those who had made contributions and sacrifices to the church. Certainly there was nothing wrong with honoring those who had made tremendous sacrifices, but I couldn't see having a church anniversary celebration of one hundred years without the Word of God. I asked them to include the Word of God in the celebration; this meant they had to change the entire format, which they did. They were willing to except the changes, and it was a wonderful church celebration. The Word of God was proclaimed in both the morning and afternoon services, and those who so rightly needed to be honored were. I remember those days like they were yesterday, and you will hear me throughout this book share some of those experiences.

The deacons were responsible for my salary. At that time, there was no housing or any other benefits, simply a salary. When I began there,

I started with a salary of $23,000, and the budget of the church was less than $100,000. There was no mention of tithes and offerings; the members simply paid dues. We soon changed the offering to include tithes and offerings.

I had a small office next to the church office, which was nicely furnished, and there I spent a great deal of time. I would arrive at the church early in the morning and leave late at night. I attended most of the ministry meetings and got to know many of the members. There were times when it was difficult to get my agenda passed because many of my ideas were new to them. I was always looking for ways to grow the church. I must admit, as I reflect back on those days, that there are probably some things I should have done differently, but my excitement for the Lord and the church kept pushing me. I soon realized I was far ahead of the leadership and knew it would take some time for them to catch up. Maybe I should have slowed down some, but again I was seeking to find ways the congregation would grow. There was no term for officers; I tried to add a few additional officers, but we still couldn't get many of the new initiatives done. There were only one or two women on the trustee board, and there were no women on the deacons' board. There was also the deacons' auxiliary, which was composed of the wives of deacons. They had very little function other than to wear white on communion Sunday.

I guess the best words to describe the early years are "growing pains." As I indicated, I cannot simply put all this on the leadership. I have to take some responsibility for my own impatience. I continually asked God to give me more patience because I knew it would take a great deal of patience to move the church forward. I believe with all my heart that that is what a pastor is to do—to take the church to another level. I was the eighth pastor, and the pastors before me had done a wonderful job in moving the church to its current level, and I thought it was my job to take them to another level.

The same year we celebrated our centennial, we started a worship service at seven thirty in the morning in addition to our service at eleven o'clock in the morning. It began on Resurrection Sunday morning of that year, and it was really a blessing. The church was full at both services, and that marked the beginning of our having more than one service. The congregation received it well; in fact, so many people loved the early service, and it was the catalyst of our growth. It meant having the choirs, along with the ushers, participate in both services, and it also strengthened the entire body of Christ. The leadership was supportive of that initiative, which gave me hope for other opportunities of growth. We reached out to a local Christian radio station and started a radio broadcast called *Visions to Victory*, which is still on today. The station was located not too far from the church, and our broadcast was on Saturday afternoons at two o'clock. Members were asked to contribute ten dollars a month to support the radio broadcast, and this they overwhelmingly did because they felt good about our church being on the radio.

If there is anything I learned in those first few years, it is that change is hard; it requires prayer and constant faith. I also learned about failures and about what to go back and seek to start over again. We did have some setbacks; some things we tried to accomplish just didn't work. I cannot say everything we sought to do in the early years was successful, but I can say we never stopped trying. We purchased some chairs for the deacons to sit on at the front of the church; that was a milestone. It might seem small to some, but for the church it raised a level of awareness of the deacons. I don't believe the chairs were a problem as much as they were a change.

One lesson I have learned is that every win isn't a win, and every loss isn't a loss. There will be times when the changes you propose will be successful from the beginning, but they may not come to fruition. On the other hand, there may be those challenges that appear to have been lost but will surface again and become victorious. Some of the ideas I couldn't push forward I realized I could bring up another way at another time. I didn't want my heart to become hardened, and I learned some valuable lessons out of those experiences. I was still in love with the church and hoped they were still in love with me.

My heart has always been for God's people so I proposed that 10 percent of our tithes and offerings would be designated to serve God's people through missions. I believe with all my heart that God has given a mandate in the Word of God in the Gospel of Matthew 25:35, "For I was hungry and you fed me, I was thirsty and you gave me a drink, I was a stranger and you invited me into your home". That was the beginning of our mission enterprise that is still in effect today; in fact, we have increased our giving to 12 percent. Our missions work would be the focal point of our ongoing ministry. Prayerfully as you share in this journey throughout these pages as a pastor or layperson, you can reflect on the changes in your congregation or, for that matter, in your own life. I'm not the same person as when I first came to the church, and Lord knows the church isn't the same. Change is good, but it is hard. I have a deeper love for the congregation now; we have grown together as I have become older. I realize how difficult change can be because change requires prayer, discipline and ones' willingness to be patient. Prayerfully I will never get to the point in my own personal life that I shut down change but just embrace and accept it as an opportunity to grow.

Chapter 15

Conflict in the Church

T his chapter is centered on the challenges that took place as a result of the growing pains in the previous chapter. Each time I tried to make a change, it bought about some challenges. Challenges aren't always bad; they can often be good. It is impossible for me to categorize the number of events that took place chronologically, but hopefully, by the Spirit of God, I will pen some of those changes that caused so much pain.

In the last chapter I spoke about the chairs for the deacons. I wish I could say that was the only incident that caused a challenge, but it was not. I vividly remember when a pastor from a neighboring church called to inform me that a member of his church, who had previously been a member here, had died and left $10,000 in his or her will for the church. I was totally excited, for this was the first member in my pastorate who had left something in his or her will for the church. The pastor, being the man of God he was, wanted to make sure we received this generous gift. Consequently, we met on several occasions, working with the attorney to bring that member's request to fruition. It was a lengthy process, but ultimately we received this wonderful gift. I might add that it is the largest gift designated in a will to our congregation by a member who left the church.

I was well aware that the trustees were the financial custodians of the church, but as pastor, I was engaged in the proceedings that led to our receiving these funds. After receiving this blessed gift and thanking members of the family along with that pastor, I spoke to the joint board, which consisted of deacons and trustees. They had knowledge of this gift prior to my receiving the check, but upon presenting the check to them and the church, I indicated that we would give a tithe of 10 percent to missions. At first they were reluctant based on some of the financial responsibilities of the church. I spoke to them from the depths of my heart and said this was a gift to our church and that we wanted to make sure it was used for people, not to pay bills or other related expenses. At no point was there anything in my heart other than honoring God by blessing His people with this gift and to give Him thanks for the spirit of the deceased person. I also brought to their minds the wonderful spirit of the pastor who had called me, even though the person who had passed was no longer a member of our church and hadn't been for a number of years. So truly the gift was a blessing.

Many of them couldn't see that, but I impressed upon them that we would provide the congregation, with a commitment from the leadership, to simply give a tithe toward missions. They continued to raise the point that I had no right to designate how the funds should be allocated. Bear in mind, I was simply seeking 10 percent of $10,000 for missions; that's just $1,000. There was little mention about giving God thanks for a gift we had no knowledge we would receive. It's amazing how we can lose sight of God's blessing just because of our own agendas. I wrote the pastor and thanked him from the bottom of my heart for what he did in allowing us to share in that benevolent gift. I also expressed thanks and gratitude to the family and to God for allowing us to sow into the lives of God's people. That incident still stands out in my heart today as to how the church moved to a higher spiritual level.

One challenge after another began to take shape and form. There were numerous opportunities granted to us to purchase property. It would take an entire chapter for me to list the wonderful opportunities God had given to us to acquire land to expand our church. One was an empty lot right next to the church; the owner approached us to see whether we would be willing to purchase that parcel of land. It sounded exciting, for in my mind I envisioned purchasing the property and enlarging the sanctuary. To enlarge the sanctuary, we would have to change its configuration, but the idea certainly was feasible.

I was naïve and really thought this would be one venture we would all agree on, for the offer really was a blessing. It was nothing but an empty lot, and we would truly have an opportunity to expand. The owner lived in the community and was successful in his career as a realtor and developer. The congregation really wrestled over acquiring this property, and the mistake I made, as I look back, was putting the cart before the horse, so to speak. I don't think they objected to purchasing the land as much as having an issue with changing the seating in the sanctuary; this would require a total change in the worship area to accommodate a new sanctuary. It was difficult for me as their pastor to get them to see how this acquisition would allow the church to grow. The owner ultimately sold the piece of property, and a home was built adjacent to the church. We lost out on a wonderful opportunity not only to acquire property but also to enlarge the sanctuary.

There was another opportunity near the railroad station, where a vacant piece of land was available. We went to the township and sought to have the plans reviewed. We hired an architect to draw some sketches. It looked like a wonderful opportunity, but again the plan fizzled because of the inability of the congregation to see the vision. They just couldn't see the church growing in that way. We spent some initial funds, and this time I really thought, in spite of some other reluctance, we were going to move forward; but we lacked the united support and failed once again to take advantage of an opportunity to grow.

We were subsequently presented with another opportunity. One of our members owned a home near the church and expressed interest in selling the property. This individual had deep roots in the church, and I really felt this time that we were going to be successful in growing the church. It was an older home on the corner facing the church with a nice landscape. This individual was a resident of the community, and I just knew this was going to be the blessing we were waiting for; this third time would be the "charm." We couldn't expand the church based on the location of the home, but we still had a great deal of interest in the property. The plans would be that it could serve as a community center, an annex to the church, a place where we could continue to do ministry and grow.

Now we faced opposition from the community, for it was said the residents didn't want to have another building on the corner of the church. I didn't understand that because it was already a house, and we were going to build a beautiful facility that would enhance the community. We had to go before the township zoning board, and we weren't successful in getting the required approval. We finally acquired the house but were unable to build anything on the property other than a home. The township complied with the residents, and it remained simply a residential property. We had the home demolished, and all we could do was use it as a parking lot. We paid an enormous amount of money for property to park cars. It is still vacant today. I have shared just three heartbreaking experiences that could have provided growth for the church and the community.

While all this was happening, there was a feeling of unrest in the community. I was sorry matters had come to this because it was a great community. I sought to convey to the congregation and the community that we would continue to be a church that was mindful of our entire community. I must admit that I was heartbroken over the failed opportunities we had for growth, but I believed God was going to work things out in the end. There was a sense of mistrust some members of the community felt toward me. I was the lead voice in all these initiatives, and people didn't like it. They made it known that I was an outsider trying to change their community. Here again, there were words like "This isn't the city" and "You're not going to make us like the city" or "Let people stay in the city and worship; we don't need them out here."

I couldn't believe those words. I was proud to be from the city and couldn't understand why such negative words were expressed. Because this was a small community, I'm sure what took place in the church meeting behind church walls soon became known to those who lived in the community. This conflict wasn't good for anyone; it wasn't good for the community and certainly not good for me. There was a widening gap that started to dampen my spirit, and I prayed like I had never prayed before. I must admit I was discouraged and literally heartbroken over our inability to adapt to change. I learned a great deal about myself and, most of all, about people and how I learned to put my trust in God. I even acknowledged some of the mistakes I had made while seeking to move the church forward. I do believe we learn a lot from our failures and successes. I made a commitment to God not to let this setback deter me from serving Him with all my heart, soul, and mind. I took time to remain still for a while and allow God to speak to my heart.

Chapter 16

Blessings for the Church

I
n the previous chapter, I shared my pain over missed opportunities for growth. I resolved that I really couldn't make any changes that would allow growth for our congregation and came to feel it was never going to happen. I resolved that it may not be in the will of God and that the church and members had literally won. Even though I had come to terms with this, I still felt somewhat discouraged and isolated, and once again I called on my pastor for words of encouragement.

Thanks be unto God that he, my family, and some members of the church told me to keep my head up and said they were praying for me. Not only were they praying for me, but they were also praying for the church, and with that behind us, we began to move forward as much as possible. There was a period of quietness in the church and the community, and there seemed to be a feeling that everything was behind us. The community had won, and members of the church were satisfied with the results, and we were doing church as usual. New members were joining, and there were no whispers or buzz in the community; things seemed to be going well. I was grateful that there was a sense of peace. I really didn't have any intentions of starting all over again; it was too painful. I just needed to move on, but sometimes God has more for us than we can even imagine.

I became somewhat content to accept what had taken place, and out of nowhere a good friend approached me and informed me that the synagogue where he served was looking to relocate. They had outgrown their site and were contemplating moving and building at a new location. He asked whether our church would consider purchasing their current place of worship. My immediate response to him was no. I just didn't want to go through that process of rejection again. It was a wonderful opportunity, with a beautiful sanctuary that would allow us to do ministry in a new and exciting way. But instead of having faith, I responded in fear: the fear of rejection, the fear of another embattlement; I just didn't believe at that point that we could achieve it, even though it was a wonderful blessing.

He told me he wasn't going to put it on the market and was going to wait for my response. I thought about it, prayed about it, and still had reservations. I knew the opportunity was God sent because we'd never had any discussion prior to this time about their relocating or our purchasing their property. We had engaged in many meaningful conversations, but never had this subject come up. I had been to their synagogue on many occasions and marveled at their wonderful facility. I never thought in my wildest dreams that it would be our future home. In our initial conversation he never spoke about the cost or a timetable; he simply asked me a question that I couldn't answer in the affirmative.

I kept asking God, "What are You doing? I've really had enough. Why this? Why now?" I have come to understand that sometimes when one door is shut, God will open another one, and in this case there were three doors shut, but now there was another door. With all my faith and trust in God, I was still reluctant. I was dwelling more on my own past hurts than on the possibilities and blessings that waited for His people.

Let me digress for a minute. I believe every pastor and leader comes to a point in their ministry when they have to ask themselves, "Is it about me?" Who wouldn't want to have a nice, large congregation and a beautiful building? If we are honest, that is something many pastors would like to have as part of their ministry. So I had to go into deep prayer not only for myself but also for our congregation.

As I mentioned, my saying no to my friend's initial request was all about me. But the more I prayed, the more God revealed to me, "It isn't for you to say no." The Lord made it clear this wasn't my initiative. I hadn't asked my friend; the opportunity was presented to me. It was a gift from God; how could I say no to what God was doing? I began to truly realize that if God is for you, He is more than the world against you. God had already covered and blessed me, and I needed to remember what He had already done and was seeking to do.

So I spoke to my friend after spending a long time with the Lord and said to him, "Let me speak to the leaders of our congregation and see whether or not it is something they would like to pursue." I knew that when I did there would be some who would really object, but more than that, I felt that the least I could do was present what God had made possible. I could write pages about my inward struggles, because I began to wonder once again about how the leadership would respond, and I knew their response was critical. These were key and influential people in the community as well as in the church. After prayer and long discussions, they agreed that we should present the proposal to the congregation.

Chapter 17

The Response from the Congregation

I called a church meeting; notice that I said "church meeting." I have since changed the name of our church meeting to "church conference," because all kinds of things have taken place at what we call a church meeting. The meeting that night was one I shall never forget. By the grace of God, there wasn't a large attendance, because word hadn't yet reached the community, so there were just a few people in attendance. Church meetings at Bethlehem were also community meetings, for people would come who weren't members of the church but had relatives who were members; some had been members at one time and still felt they had a large say to what was taking place. So with a small group of people, much to my surprise after a lengthy discussion, we moved forward to explore the purchase of the synagogue.

Going forward, our theme and vision was simply, "The church is in prayer as we explore a new house of worship." A small group of leaders of the joint ministry met with leaders of the synagogue to discuss purchasing the property. We discovered in our relationship with the synagogue that the president of the synagogue carried a lot of weight. This didn't take away from the leadership of the rabbi, for the congregation was empowered to elect a president who would oversee their finances and administrative work.

The president of the synagogue was very supportive of our interest in the acquisition of their property. They didn't have a timeline because they hadn't completed the purchase of their new property. They were visionary people and wanted to make sure their current synagogue wouldn't be in competition with another synagogue located close to them. In my humble view, I believe even now that their concept of not being close to another synagogue and how that would take away their ability to grow is worthwhile exploring. Far too often we have one church after another competing for the same congregant as opposed to looking at areas in which we aren't so close in proximity. To me that was a good, sound business decision.

We may not talk about it much, but the church is a business and must be run with sound biblical principles. I have learned a great deal from our Jewish brothers and sisters about building, planning, and using the gifts of the congregations. Their main desire to build came out of the fact that as spacious as their facility was, it didn't accommodate all their needs, particularly on High Holidays. I might add that ultimately they moved less than five miles away, so some of the myths and stereotypes about our Jewish brothers and sisters are simply a myth. It is ironic that even as we sought to relocate, there were those who said we were moving out of our neighborhood. As I mentioned earlier, the neighborhood of our church was predominantly an African-American community, and the new location was a much more affluent and totally different neighborhood. So in our conversation with the synagogue leaders, we became aware of their need to relocate and why they thought of us initially. We had developed a relationship, and I had come to know members of the synagogue, and they had come to know us. This connection created a strong bond between men and women of faith.

They proposed a price for the synagogue of more than $3.5 million with no exact timetable in mind. By any stretch of an imagination, $3.5 million seemed large to our congregation at that point, but larger still was moving into a synagogue out of the community. We had little reserve, and yet there was within me a passion to move forward. We used the word *explore*, so again it wasn't something concrete; we were just looking at the possibilities. Questions were raised, such as, "Where were we going to get the money?" and "What will we do with the current site?" These were all questions I couldn't answer. As I think back on that evening, even though there was a small attendance, I am convinced that those who voted to "explore" were simply just for that; they didn't desire to purchase but to "explore." There were so many unknowns as well as so many naysayers still hanging around.

Word hadn't really reached the community yet, even about this whole matter of exploring, but as time went on, even the word *explore* made some people angry. Little by little their voices began to be heard and got the attention of those in the community. Letters were written to the editor of the local newspaper. This newspaper, which was printed once a week, became the voice of those who were disgruntled. It wasn't simply one letter but sometimes two and three letters to the editor regarding our exploring the sale of the synagogue. The newspaper didn't edit the letters; they simply printed what the people wrote. So in the midst of all this, synagogue officials asked me whether our members were in support of purchasing their property, because they didn't want to become engaged in a battle with our congregation. I pondered how we could move in spite of this negative press and unfair criticism leveled at me; this was just the beginning, and it grew worse over time.

Without any kind of agreement in hand, we prayed about doing a capital campaign to raise some funds and indicate to the synagogue that we were serious about exploring the purchase of their property. We contacted several businesses and ministries that specialized in biblical fund-raising and finally settled on one group after hearing many presentations. They made a wonderful presentation to the leadership of the church, and we ultimately shared that with the congregation. We paid them around $40,000 to lead us in a capital campaign to raise $2 million over three years for the purchase of the site. They had a very detailed plan that required a lot of church participation.

We had to find someone in the church who would lead this capital campaign, and after much prayer, I asked a faithful couple whether they would chair this awesome responsibility. He had previously served as chairperson of the trustee ministry, and they were very committed to the life of our congregation. They both had some strong administrative qualities, gifts, and knowledge that earned the respect from our congregation, and I felt they could provide the kind of leadership the church needed for this endeavor. To my knowledge this was the first stewardship effort of this magnitude in the life of Bethlehem and certainly in my ministry.

We needed more than one hundred families for this plan to really work. Bear in mind that we didn't have an agreement when we started or knew what we would be doing with the new site, and there were still rumblings and discord in the community. These took a toll on the church, but we moved forward. The group conducted training and orientation with levels of leadership all under the direction of the lead couple; there were dinners at members' homes, where members were asked to make a pledge to the capital campaign. I remember when we were advised to make sure to acknowledge our top givers so they would be a source of inspiration to others. The leadership was asked to give first, and the overall effort wasn't equal giving but equal sacrifice. The smallest donation to the largest would be of value, and no one's gift would be too small to be recognized.

Can you imagine how difficult it was to try to have this campaign around stewardship when there were so much confusion and disharmony in the church? We pressed on. The night we had our kickoff dinner, which was part of the overall capital campaign thrust, we received more than $1.5 million in pledges.

With all this, we still didn't have an agreement; all we had was an act of faith and the word from the president of the synagogue that they were still interested in selling us the facility, in spite of what they were hearing and seeing. For the first time, I, along with others, made a substantial sacrificial offering to the capital campaign. My offering was truly an act of faith, because at that time I really didn't have the funds in hand, but I had God in my heart. I watched people give sacrificially, and the enthusiasm and spirit in the church were great. God sent me encouragers and fellow believers, and I trusted that God was going to open up this door. I didn't know exactly when that door would be opened, but I felt that God was still working. Those were wonderful moments because many relationships were made between pastor and people. We learned to pray together, and my own faith, strength, and confidence in God grew.

I discovered God in a new way. I sometimes drove by the synagogue and gave God thanks for what was about to happen. We even gathered some members together and walked around the synagogue seven times, using the number seven from the Word of God. I realized God was going to take our congregation to another level. I was tested on every hand. There was even a period when we didn't receive new members. We even had several members leave, but the campaign kept on going. We probably received about 75 percent of the pledges, and still there was no agreement. The synagogue was very cautious about not signing anything until they were sure about everything. I've come to value another business decision from them; their faith was strong, but they were savvy about their business transactions. They ran into some problems of their own with their land development, and they didn't want to commit to anything until they got their final okay.

It became a waiting game, and finally we were able to agree and sign a tentative agreement with many clauses in place. Once again, there were those who balked at signing a temporary agreement, but I had confidence in our leadership and knew I could trust not only the rabbi but also the leadership of his synagogue. The Word of God is true in Romans 8:31, "...If God is for us, who can ever be against us?" After a long, tedious battle with the synagogue, with acquiring its land, and with their building just about constructed, we made an agreement for the sale of the property, but it wasn't over yet. As you continue to read, remember, "It's not where you start but where you finish that counts."

Chapter 18

Preparing for Settlement

A s we moved closer to purchasing the synagogue, the chair of the capital campaign became ill. He and his wife did an extraordinary job in moving the church to another spiritual level in our giving. His sickness was very severe, and we sought God's healing for him and strength for his wife. As mentioned previously, there were a lot of tiers in leadership, but we needed someone willing to step up to the plate and carry out this awesome responsibility of receiving the pledges so we could be in the position to make the purchase.

As the Lord worked it out, our youngest son and his wife accepted the challenge, and they did a remarkable job. How proud I was as my son and daughter picked up the mantle to move our church forward. He would often quote from the Word of God in Luke 12:48, "To whom much is given, much is required." He used that to indicate how God had blessed their marriage and their careers, and he wanted to give back. They were a young couple, and the bigger challenge was that they were the pastor's son and daughter, but they never used their relationship with their father as a springboard. God was the source of their foundation, and they made it clear that this wasn't about their father, the pastor; it was all about God. My heart was overjoyed as members of the congregation received and supported them. They continued to lift up the former campaign leader in prayer, and the congregation was challenged never to forget the tremendous leadership they had provided. The prayers of God's people were answered, and he made a wonderful recovery. They once again became a vital part of this God-given initiative.

We moved closer to the time we would make settlement. God had spoken, and in spite of all the obstacles, and there were many, we stood on the dawn of a wonderful blessing. Our church, Bethlehem Baptist Church, The House of Bread, and Congregation Beth Or, The House of Light, were getting closer to becoming truly bread and light. We could see the light at the end of the tunnel, and we knew God was blessing us with our daily bread. The bread of life had sustained us, and His light had guided us over some rough rocky days, but we have come this far by faith, leaning on the Lord. We applied for and were granted a mortgage. Many thought this would be impossible, but God made it possible. What a marvelous blessing it was to experience the hand of God working, through our church and the synagogue, even though our church and the synagogue were a short distance apart. In many ways they were a long distance apart—not so much by miles but by faith, tears, and challenges. You could walk from our neighborhood to the synagogue, realizing distance doesn't always determine one's journey; faith does.

The journey to purchase the synagogue was never about me; it was always about "the blessings of God". There was joy down in my soul as we moved closer to this God-given opportunity. Our settlement was set for a Monday morning, and I received word on the Friday before that the synagogue was going to press for a one-hundred-year lease agreement. The word reached our leadership, and that Sunday after the worship service, I was informed that they were never going to accept a one-hundred-year lease from the synagogue; in fact, they made it very clear they wouldn't go to settlement on Monday.

Once again my heart was broken. We had come so close and yet were so far away. No longer was it just the community, but this was the leadership; these were the individuals who supported me, prayed for me, stood by me, and now were abandoning me. I couldn't believe our leadership, who had made sacrifices in their giving, time, and talents, were now going to quit, resolving not to go any further. I wish I could put into words the lump in my throat and in my gut, and the pain in my heart. I didn't know exactly what to do, and I didn't want to lash out at them, for they had been very supportive. There were the few who had believed in me and the ability God had given us to purchase this property. They had been to my home and broken bread with us. We'd laughed and cried together; we'd shared this journey, and they had made sacrifices, yet now they were about to walk away. I heard things like, "You and your friend, the rabbi," and all kinds of murmurs. I was literally in tears. I asked them to meet me at the church at five o'clock that evening. I didn't know what I was going to say or how I would be received. I went home after church for a brief period of time, but I couldn't wait until the five o'clock hour. I left my home around two in the afternoon, went into the sanctuary at church, got down on my knees, and talked to God like I had never talked to Him before. I asked God to strengthen me and give me wisdom and discernment, for I knew that after all we had been through, God hadn't brought us this far for us to turn around. I had to find some way to convince the leadership this was all God's plan.

I stayed in the sanctuary until five, when I met with the leadership. They were very determined that they weren't going to engage in a one-hundred-year lease under any circumstances. They pointed out that it was unreasonable, and they were adamant that they were going to simply walk away from this agreement of sale. At that point I pleaded with them to think about what God had done in the midst of this entire journey. I then said to them, "Do you really believe the synagogue would be indebted to us for one hundred years?" I knew the synagogue had their challenges with the land development, but I also knew they had made a great financial investment in this property, and they wanted very much to continue in this sound business arrangement. The rabbi, whom I trusted completely, had also assured me that there was no intention at all for them to hold us to a one-hundred-year lease. My relationship with him had grown, and I trusted him completely, since he was a man of integrity and honesty.

After several hours of prayer and pleading, they agreed to go to settlement. I got home that evening and once again fell on my knees and thanked God for the blessings of the day. It was a day full of challenges. I remembered, as I was praying the words of my pastor, "This is the day the Lord has made, let us rejoice and be glad in it. Life is sometimes unfair, but God is good all the time." Certainly God was good that day and every day.

I woke up the next morning, knowing it was also a day full of mercy; as recorded in Lamentations 3:22-23, "… morning by morning new mercies we see". We saw God's mercy come to pass that Monday morning as we made settlement. We sat at the table—Jew and gentile, rabbi and preacher, brothers and sisters of faith—and signed an agreement to purchase the synagogue. My soul was singing my favorite hymn entitled "It is Well With My Soul", the words recorded in the hymn are:

> When peace like a river, attendeth my way,
> When sorrows like sea billows role
> Whatever my lot, thou hast taught me to say
> It is well, it is well, with my soul.

My soul was set on fire, since we had accomplished the first part of this incredible journey for the glory of God. I forgot all about the bumper stickers, the posters, the letters to the editors, and just began to praise God. We hugged each other, shed some tears with each other, and gathered for prayer. What a mighty God we serve. Once again just remember: it's not where you start but where you finish that counts.

Chapter 19

Waiting for Moving Day

We moved into our new place of worship in April 2006. It was a historical day; we now have one church with two locations. Our prayers had been answered, and there was a great deal of excitement. Many renovations were made in preparing for this glorious day. We added a choir loft and baptismal pool in the sanctuary, and we upgraded the media equipment. The synagogue removed all their stained-glass windows, and we installed close to thirty windows, each of which depicted a story in the Bible, at a cost of $3,500 apiece. The church spent well over $1 million in renovations, including the pastor's office, the church office, and the many rooms and classrooms. To this day, there is no indication that our new place of worship was a synagogue. The synagogue presented us with a wonderful gift of a stained glass window of the burning bush, which we have hung in our café.

We began to refer to our new place as the Spring House Worship Center, still keeping our original site. Many of those in opposition to our moving decided not to continue their membership, but we continued to grow as new members came to experience worship at our new house of worship. It really was a community of believers working to make sure our opening would give glory to God and edify the people of God. Countless hours were spent preparing for worship that day. My pastor preached the dedication service in the afternoon, and it was a day I shall never forget as long as I live. We were able to realize this God-given dream in our new facility, which had once been a home, then a synagogue, and now the new house of worship for our church. Through all the tears, struggles, pain, and disappointment, God had truly blessed us.

As I look back over that experience, I can say without hesitation or reservation that it was worth it all; put in another expression, I wouldn't take anything for my journey. I gained so much strength and faith as a result of relying on the Lord. Our church long after me will be a beacon light in this community. I shall always be indebted to my rabbi friend, colleague, and brother; and the members of the synagogue who didn't waver in their commitment to sell to us in spite of all the obstacles. It is a wonderful feeling when you are able to see your dreams unfold. As I have indicated through the title of this book, *It's Not Where You Start but Where You Finish That Counts*, there were many opportunities for us to throw in the towel, but we stayed true to our Lord. As a result, we are still giving God thanks for our new place of worship. That memorable day still resides in my heart. My pastor preached a powerful sermon, and the choir from my home church blessed us with hymns and songs of praise. There were several public officials present, and for the first time in a long time, we received glowing reports in our local newspaper.

I'm grateful for the support of my wife, sons, and daughters during that difficult time. They were as equally grateful to God for this day that had come to past. There are milestones in one's ministry, and this was truly one in mine and hopefully one in the life of our congregation. More than one hundred years ago, nineteen founders stepped out in faith and established a church called Bethlehem, and now, years later, we added to that foundation, keeping God as our foundation. I have learned that with God for you, He is more than the world against you. Someone once said that what God has for you is for you. I could write pages of what it took to get us to this point. I have said to the congregation on many occasions that it was never about me but all about God.

For God to bless a predominantly African-American congregation in the heart of Montgomery County, one of the riches counties in our state, is truly a remarkable blessing. During the days that followed that dedication service, I literally walked around the six and a half acres of landscape, with such beautiful scenery and green grass. The place reminded me of the words recorded in Psalm 24:1, "The earth is the Lord's, and everything in it. The World and all its people belong to Him". I must admit that I still find it hard to comprehend why anyone would be opposed to such a beautiful facility. The sanctuary is marvelous and so conducive for worship; when the sunlight shines through the stained-glass windows, you feel the presence of the Lord all around. It is spacious and has many rooms that are used for study and fellowship. We were successful in getting a local company to refurbish a nursery, and we use it for our young children on Sunday mornings. We have three floors, and each has sufficient meeting rooms. We are blessed to house interfaith families for an entire month annually; they literally stay in the church. God has given us so many opportunities, and we have sought to take advantage of each and every one of them.

As a way to compromise and/or find common ground with our former community, we put in place a plan to have three services, one at the old site at 7:30 a.m. and at our new site at 9:30 a.m. and 11:15 a.m. I would practically run from one site to the other each Sunday for the 9:30 a.m. worship service, simply trying to continue healing. We continued the three services for several years and then made the decision to move to having the two services just at our new facility. We were successful in getting another congregation to lease our old house of worship. They were extremely happy to have a place of worship, and we were grateful the site would be used. We had a verbal commitment with that congregation that if any of our members wanted to have their service at the old site, we would be able to accommodate them so that their final wishes of being laid to rest was at what they called the "home place." We did as much as we could to continually reach out to the community and let them know they were a vital part of our ministry. It worked for a period of time, and there were times when they wanted to make a statement, so they would have a home-going service for a family member there and request another pastor to do the eulogy. Once again,

I tried to take the high road, but it didn't change their minds of whom they wanted to do their funeral service.

We also had some challenges with the township at our new location. We wanted to erect a digital sign, indicating the name of the church, but we found real opposition, since the township is very strict about signs in a residential area. We had to compromise and ultimately received permission for a sign in keeping with the regulations of the township. That was just one obstacle we had with the township, and over the years the relationship has improved tremendously. I remembered that we had signage at our former site, which was in a predominantly African-American community, and couldn't understand why that same kind of signage couldn't be at our new site. I didn't want to bring up race issues and then realized we were in a totally different environment.

The cost of the homes increased greatly at our new location, and we had to be sensitive to the residents in the community. I didn't need another battle; I was battle fatigued. I have learned the real meaning of persistence, humility, faith, and integrity. I praise God today that during that entire journey, the Lord protected me and kept my body strong, for those were days when I could have had a stroke or heart attack, but by the grace of God, He protected me. I am still rejoicing over the blessings God has given as I sit in my office now and pen these words. I feel like leaping with joy. So many wonderful things have taken place in the life of this congregation since the dedication day. We have had so many services we couldn't have held previously. We have had college choirs; the Martin Luther King Jr. Memorial Award Services, for which we are able to accommodate more than one thousand attendees; weddings; and baptisms.

I'm grateful to God for those pastors who have built strong congregations and new edifices; there is always a price to be paid, but the blessings far outweigh the price. I believe it isn't about the building, and I know with all my heart that God's house should be a place of beauty. Why would we want God's house to be anything less than our homes? Our God deserves the very best. I'm grateful for the leadership of this church as they have truly invested in making additional improvements and renovations. I am always mindful of the house of God when I go into a restroom, since I believe a restroom represents a lot about a congregation. Appearance has a lot of value. Members who continue to work hard in the church really exemplify their love for the Lord. But as much as we place value in the building, it doesn't supersede what we give for missions and the work of the kingdom. The next chapter will speak about the work of the kingdom and our commitment to home and foreign missions as well as charitable causes.

Chapter 20

Mission Initiatives

As our church grew spiritually and financially, we put in place that 10 percent of our giving through tithes and offerings would be allotted to missions. This was radical for our church, for we'd never thought about or even acted on giving one-tenth to the work of the kingdom in the mission field. We have currently moved to allot 12 percent, with a continuing effort to raise it to at least 15 percent. When we began, we saw the hand of God moving, and we began to realize the needs of God's people on the foreign mission field as well as at home. Because our church is duly aligned, in that we belong to American Baptist Churches as well as the National Baptist Convention, we sought to give generously to each of them. Not only that, but we saw missions as being far beyond simply our church affiliation; rather, we saw many other charitable causes that touched the lives of God's people.

Our support for the American Cancer Society over the years has been part of our ministry. For a number of years, we have observed Cancer Awareness Sunday by lifting up cancer patients and families, and supporting Praise for the Cure. As one who has experienced the loss of loved ones as the result of cancer, I have become increasingly aware of the need for the church to be engaged in the fight against this disease. Our goal has always been to have a holistic ministry across religious and denominational lines. Early on in my ministry, which continues today, we supported the Interfaith Housing Alliance and contributed a significant amount of dollars to support one of their apartments in our community, which provides housing for families in transition. We have come to appreciate transitional housing, and many families have been helped to regain hope and healing as a result of having a warm place to live. We have also housed families in our congregation for more than twenty years as a part of our outreach ministry with Interfaith Housing Alliance.

For nearly ten years, we have given $10,000 to Children's Hospital for Sickle Cell. This initiative was started as the result of a family in our church whose son has sickle cell, and this family has been raising awareness and funds for a number of years. As a church we are committed to stand with them and help other families. Our commitment to healthy living allowed us to make a sizable contribution to the YMCA to support families in need with counseling, day care, and financial assistance. I remember how our congregation responded to Hurricane Katrina when we gave over $40,000 to American Baptist Churches. There were many other catastrophes for which we raised monies through missions, all for the glory of God.

We now have a home in Kenya, East Africa, our Ogada Children's Home, where we support over 100 children on a monthly basis for their day-to-day needs. We have literally spent thousands of dollars in refurbishing their home, helping to provide water for their personal and physical needs. We have made several trips to Africa, all in line with our missions initiatives. We have worked closely with Chosen 300, a ministry that operates in the city and throughout the world in providing food for those in need. When we started some years ago, our ministry was defined as Feeding the Homeless, but as a way to provide more dignity and honor to those who live in the streets, we simply changed the name from Feeding the Homeless to Gifted to Serve. We haven't wavered in our commitment to make a difference in the lives of God's people. We adopted the Kinsey School in Philadelphia by providing supplies, computers, tutoring, and counseling to many of our students, whom we see as gifted. Unfortunately, Kinsey was one of the schools closed, but we still keep those children close to our hearts.

The numbers of outreach ministries we have supported and continue to support are numerous. We have opened a food pantry that provides food to families and offers a "compassionate closet," where clothes are available to those in need. We actually refurbished several rooms to house these outreach ministries. Our commitment to home and foreign missions is seen through our support to American Baptist Churches and the National Baptist Convention as they make appeals in times of crisis and/or need. Our ongoing support for the American Red Cross and Salvation Army and some local organizations in our region are opportunities God has given to us to touch the hearts of God's people. We see this mandate to missions in the Gospel of Matthew 25:35: "For I was hungry and you fed me, I was thirsty and you gave me something to drink, I was a stranger and you invited me into your home." We understand this isn't an option but a mandate, and we continue to seek to carry out that mandate by loving God and serving people.

Our mission at our church to love God and serve His people is not only marked on the walls of the church but also dwells in the hearts of God's people. Our desire is to be known as a church where the people of God are cared for, loved, and supported in ways that really reflect our true commitment to God. Our benevolence, supported by our deacons' ministry, is also part of our initiatives for mission. I cannot even begin to count the number of dollars we have allocated to helping families, all part of God's mission for His people. This isn't confined to simply members of our congregation but rather to those in need. I believe God has granted us His favor because we are committed to the lives of His people. This may be radical for some because there are those who define missions as simply that which relates to the Christian enterprise, but I maintain that missions work is far greater than those who simply are part of the church or, for that matter, isn't even related to the church in terms of the cause. One of the blessings I am grateful for comes out of the fact that the congregation as a whole isn't concerned about what's in it for them. In other words we aren't doing this to gain members; we are doing this because it is God's will.

We have another agenda, the kingdom agenda. We are always looking for new ways to help God's people. The United Negro College Fund, No Place for Hate, the Jewish Defense League, and the NAACP are just a few of the civil rights organizations we support. As I mentioned, for charitable causes, we support the Walk for Aids and Alzheimer's Association, and we give toward diabetes and those illnesses that affect one's life. I remember discussions as to whether we should give to foreign or home missions. Our choice isn't one or the other; it's both. Not only is it both, but so are other causes I mentioned and many more. The church budget must always reflect giving to missions. When you look at the church budget, you can see where our priorities are.

I work with many nonprofit organizations, and their commitment is that salaries, utilities, and other expenses do not supersede the commitment to serve the people who benefit from the nonprofit. In other words, the church must be about the business of the church. Giving is a part of worship. I am also truly grateful that we aren't bogged down as a church about ideology or theology matters that prevent us from truly giving. We have come a long way in terms of our commitment to the lives of people through our mission efforts, but we still have a long way to go. I maintain that the government cannot do it all; in fact, we learn that the government won't and isn't going to do it all. The church must be at the forefront of all of God's people, supporting our children in school as we see schools close, providing our children with nutritional food to begin their day, and helping with housing and family needs.

We even go as far as supporting, through our mission efforts, counseling for married couples and families who do not have insurance; we see that as a valued part of our commitment to God. We have even provided, through our missions efforts, the burial costs for a family member when there is no insurance. As you read this chapter, you will see that mission effort isn't defined by one simple act, but it is all inclusive. Our passion or commitment is to make a difference in what God has called us to do and be.

We are truly a missions-minded people. To see the church grow spiritually is to see them sow in the lives of others. I believe with all my heart that God has blessed our church with His favor because we have sought to honor Him by caring for others. When I begin to list some of the blessings of ministry in these last thirty years, I see that our commitment to missions stands out far above any other accomplishments. To see how people have embraced this whole matter of giving and serving is incredible. We are still in the midst of trying to make a difference.

Chapter 21

Compassionate Home

I n the later part of 2014, a neighbor living next to our church knocked on my office door and indicated she was going to sell her home. She asked whether our church would be interested in purchasing it. I was amazed because this was exactly what had taken place years ago when my rabbi friend indicated to me that the synagogue was selling its building and asked whether we would be interested in purchasing it. I immediately felt the movement of God. I spoke to our leadership, and their response was overwhelmingly in support of our pursuing this property, unlike when we purchased this church building and there were challenges in the congregation.

In this instance, there was full agreement that we should make every effort to purchase this home. There were two and a half acres of land and a home at a cost of more than $500,000. The trustees did due diligence and moved forward with haste. The congregation was asked to pledge so we were able to show our commitment to a lending institution. On July 4, 2014, the holiday weekend, we asked the congregation to respond and give $50,000. The response was overwhelming; the congregation responded with well over $70,000. My heart was overjoyed. After some negotiations we made an agreement and were successful in getting a mortgage. We needed approval from the township to purchase the property, since it was zoned as residential, and would now be part of our church.

Once again we were blessed with no opposition. Our neighbors were supportive as well as the officials in the township. We continued to feel the movement of God as we prayed for this land to be used for the glory of God. I just marveled at how God was blessing our congregation, for on April 2, 2006, we moved into our present sanctuary; and nine years later, on April 12, 2015, we dedicated our new home to the glory of God.

After much prayer and suggestions from the congregation, we named our new home our Compassionate Home and the surrounding garden, the Martin Luther King Jr. Garden, in memory of the legacy and work of Rev. Dr. Martin Luther King Jr. The service of dedication was incredible. A close friend and pastor brought the message, and we were blessed to have public officials in attendance, who offered words of congratulations. As a result of God's granting us this magnificent blessing, we committed to give $100,000 to missions. Never in the life of our church have we committed that significant of an amount as a single act, but as before, we believe in the scripture recorded in Luke 12:48, "When someone has been given much, much will be required in return; and when someone has been entrusted with much, even more will be required". Once again, the church responded in such a marvelous way through acts of kindness.

Renovations are under way to beautify our home and create a place where people will know that we love God and serve people. I never thought in my wildest dreams that we would have nine acres of beautiful property in one of the richest counties in our state. I can only imagine how those nineteen founders, who stepped out on faith 126 years ago and established a church, would have felt to see that same church thriving. Those nineteen African-Americans worked so hard during difficult days: days of slavery, depression, and oppression. How would they feel to now see a multicultural church where people from all walks of life are serving God?

The initiative of acts of kindness was really developed during the Lenten season, and we have committed to give $100,000 to missions. I was blessed to watch a TV talk show personality, Steve Harvey, whom I have come to love and appreciate. He expresses openly how God continues to blessed him, and because of his commitment to give back, our church developed a forty-day calendar of acts of kindness. Each day we were challenged to do a small act of love for someone else without any recognition. This expression of love demonstrated once again our loving God and our service to people. The Lenten season didn't end our acts of kindness, but it was just the beginning. This also led us to name our new home a place where ministry can unfold, people's lives are changed, and we serve people throughout our community. I keep remembering over and over again that it's not where you start but where you finish that counts.

We have come a mighty long way by the hand of God. It is God's hand that led us. I am just a vessel in His hands. All that we have achieved or ever will achieve is because of God. I am grateful that God has used me in some way to serve His people. Long after I've gone home to glory, this church will stand as a beacon light to this dark world. I am, along with this present congregation, a recipient of those who came before us. Hopefully, we will leave something behind that the next generation will contribute to. We know this isn't the last chapter in the life of our church or, for that matter, in my own life. I believe with all my heart that the best is best to come. There are blessings awaiting all of us when we put our trust and faith in God. I'm standing on tiptoes, waiting for God to make the next move.

I know God has more in store—not just for me but for all His people. I have tried to say throughout this entire book that this story isn't about me or about our church; it's all about God. It's amazing how God can take one whose life has been torn and tattered and restore them to wholeness.

Chapter 22

Church Without Walls

I n 2011, one of the ministers who had united with our church approached me, expressing to me that his previous church had a prayer line. This concept wasn't new to me or our church, since for a number of years we had a Dial a Prayer Line. A telephone number was available for persons to call and receive a prerecorded prayer. However, as the result of technology, it became obsolete, and there were other opportunities for persons to call and engage in prayer.

I must admit that in many congregations, including ours, prayer isn't always as vibrant as it used to be. I remember that while growing up, we would have a midweek prayer service. People would spend an hour or more just in praying and praising God, and this was sometimes followed by Bible study. Many congregations have moved away from prayer services and have a midweek Bible study, which sometimes includes preaching and teaching.

At our church, because we no longer have a neighborhood church and many members live an hour or more away, it is difficult to have two hours of services during the week, particularly with young families. We have sought to have early-morning worship before the service on Sundays, but that has been sporadic. I have always looked at new ways for prayer to be a vital part of our ministry, since I believe prayer is the foundation of our ministry. With that in mind and with a challenge to bring new life to our prayer ministry, I was intrigued to begin this new prayer line. The minister indicated in our initial conversation that people would call in and pray, sing songs, and testify.

So we began a prayer line from six thirty to seven o'clock in the morning. It started with about ten people; it was slow in the beginning as it encouraged people to pray early in the morning as they prepared to go to work or get their children ready for school. We provided a toll-free number that allowed people from across the country to call in. I soon realized that many other congregations have similar services, but many have just one moderator, with only the host doing the praying and the callers listening. Sometimes having only the host is necessary because of the volume of people who may call, but the Lord led me to have the callers participate and offer their prayers. This step has proved to be a challenge because we ask callers to put their phones on mute when they aren't praying to alleviate interference or interruption. We have had all kinds of interferences, such as snoring, the sound of a radio or TV in the background, and the noise of someone in the midst of cooking breakfast or doing something else, but we have persevered. The songwriter says, "Our good days outweigh our bad days, we won't complain."

We have had more good days with little or no interruption, and the prayer line has really become a blessing—so much so that we moved from ten callers to around forty to fifty every day. We then increased the prayer time an additional fifteen minutes from 6:15 to 7:00 a.m. I have been blessed to host it five days a week, and another church member, one of our associate ministers, has been faithful to host it on Saturdays and Sundays. I thank God that I've never missed a day due to illness; I have missed due to being on vacation or attending a convention.

I've watched in amazement how this service has grown; starting out as a prayer line, it has grown spiritually and numerically. My life has been truly blessed to watch God work in the lives of His people. We have witnessed healing, reconciliation, and comfort; and we have even seen souls won for Christ. We have prayed for our entire nation for thirty-one days; we have had calls from our orphanage in Kenya, South Africa; people from all over the nation have called in from Arizona, Delaware, New York, and Chicago. And the Spirit of God has led us to name this wonderful early-morning experience our early-morning worship service. Persons of different denominations and ethnicities gather together for this hour of power. I said "hour" because we have again changed the time; it is now six to seven o'clock.

What a wonderful blessing it is to wake up in the morning and see the beauty of God unfolding as we gather to give God praise. This early-morning worship service gave me a blessed inspiration to write a daily devotional for our members. These devotions are made available to the people of God; a devotion that flows from the heart of God can be received online or in paperback form. Devotions are written on a quarterly basis, and much of the inspiration has come from hosting the early-morning worship service. God has granted me an opportunity to pastor a congregation from across the country. I've come to know God's people by their voices, their prayers, the songs they sing, and their testimonies.

To see the beauty of God working early in the morning is incredible. One of the members of the early-morning worship service sent me a card I have in my office; the words read in this manner: "When you open your eyes this morning, God has already taken care of every unfolding detail of your day." How true that is, for as the hymn says, "Morning by morning new mercies I see." To begin your day in prayer by giving God your first fruits of the day gives you the assurance that no matter what happens in that day, you have the blessings of God with you. I never imagined that we would grow together across geographical lines, which allow us to share some of the deep and intimate places of our hearts without fear of judgment. They have been honest and transparent, and our lives have been made so much better.

I do not consider it a burden to wake up in the morning at five to be a part of the early-morning worship service. It isn't a chore or a burden; it is a blessing. I have met so many wonderful servants of God, men and women who aren't ashamed to praise God. We have gone through summer, winter, spring, and fall; and we have seen God through it all. We have cried together, shared joys and sorrows together, and felt the hand of God moving. One of the most fascinating aspects about the early-morning worship device is that there is no division, just people willing to praise God. I've felt the prayers of God's people giving me strength, and I continually remind this congregation that it's not about our church or me; the hand of God has brought all of us together.

I met one of our prayer warriors' daughters, who is waiting for an organ donation. I call her name almost every day. Her faith is incredible, and I feel like I've known her for years. There are so many others I have come to know in that same way. God has broken down some of the walls that sometimes separate us. I would invite you to join us by calling 1-641-715-3655, participant access code 674854. Please remember to hit *6 to put your phone on mute. I don't known how many times I have said that, but I do ask callers to have their hearts open to God. I don't know anything better than to wake up each morning and join in the early-morning worship service.

I have also said to this congregation, "This isn't a substitute for worship." I encourage them to worship with their congregation and, if they do not have a congregation, to find one. I also encourage them not to see this as a substitute for their private or personal prayer but as an opportunity to join together with one another in prayer. The Word of God says, in Matthew 18:19, "Again, truly I tell you that if two of you on earth agree about anything they ask for, it will be done for them by my Father in heaven".

The Holy Spirit is on the line, the movement of God is felt, and there is a spirit of God that is present as we gather for worship. Something happens to put joy in our hearts, peace in our minds, and pep in our step. I thank God for technology; yes, I know sometimes it is used in the wrong way, but technology is truly a blessing. People can call from their cell phone or in the car by using Bluetooth. We can connect with one another all across the country.

I would encourage you to join us one morning; your day will be better, your life will be better, and you may find yourself wanting to become a part of this daily blessing. The members of the early-morning worship service have also connected to our church ministry. They took part in acts of kindness as we offered ourselves to someone else every day. I give God praise for this wonderful ministry. Prayer takes place not just in the sanctuary but in the confines of our homes each and every day.

There have been times when we have even had an early-morning worship service other than first thing in the morning. We have had a home-going service for two of our faithful prayer warriors who have gone on to glory, Christmas Eve, New Year's Eve, and Resurrection Sunday Sunrise Service. To watch this service grow from just an idea to become a reality has been amazing; we now average one hundred callers for our hour of power. Where there is no vision, the people perish. I'm even looking forward to when we can have FaceTime on the early-morning worship service so we can see the faces of those whose voices we hear every morning. As one of our faithful members sang,

> It is no secret to what God can do
> What He has done for others He can do for us too.

Just remember, it's not where you start but where you finish that counts.

Chapter 23

Goals and Visions

When I celebrated my thirtieth pastoral anniversary, I shared with our congregation some of the goals and visions God had granted me. This followed the message "Magnificent Obsession," which my pastor preached. As he preached with eloquence, he spoke about obsession in a positive way. The Spirit of God moved me about my being obsessed with wanting to serve the Lord continually. In that sermon, he also indicated that God doesn't call us to be successful; more importantly, He wants us to be faithful. When one is obsessed, he or she moves, sometimes even alone, not having fear of failure.

I recently had a conversation with one of my colleagues; being transparent and vulnerable, I expressed that I wanted God to let me know when it's time for me to step aside from pastoring. Yet, on the other hand, I don't want to leave before my time. I wouldn't go ahead of God, but rather God would lead me to continually lead our congregation. I believe with all my heart that every pastor ought to have passion, integrity, and commitment as he serves God's people. The passion I have still runs deep in my soul, and I am eager to follow God as He leads me. I want to see our church grow spiritually, even deeper than we are now, and for the power of God to heighten our own individual lives.

I have sought to move this 128-year-old predominantly African-American congregation to become a multicultural church. My heart's desire is for us to break down some of the walls that exist along racial and even denominational lines. There is so much turmoil in the world with racism sexism and classism that the church must be the conduit for change. We cannot expect the government or corporate America to do what the church is called to do. I look back at the changes that have come to our congregation, with women in ministry, our Ogada home, our new Compassionate Home—all requiring conviction and faith.

I also believe that where there is no vision, the people will perish. God doesn't give the vision without provision. We have grown together as a congregation, and no longer do I feel that I am alone as I seek to lead these people. The leadership of this church has embraced what God has given to me; consequently, the congregation feels it and has embraced it. My dream is connected to my goals that the new home we purchased will become an extension of the ministry at our church.

There is one additional home adjacent to our property, and I pray it will become ours at some point. This would truly allow us to enlarge our territory and own valuable real estate that can be used for the glory of God. My dream is that our growth won't be relegated to numbers but rather to a deeper commitment of God's people that will allow us to really see the reality of loving God and serving people come to fruition. We can explore additional outreach ministries to comfort those who are grieving, a hospice ministry in the life of the church, and ministries that touch the lives of God's people in every phase and facet of life. I pray to get to the point and time when the Lord has spoken, in terms of my retirement, that the church will embrace a man or woman who will continue to carry out the vision of this church so we won't go backward but forward; and I also pray that they would grant me the opportunity to be involved with my successor in some way. I also pray that our church will continue to be that light, the bread of life, that souls might be saved. I could write countless pages of how inspired I am in my desire to see the glory of God manifested in the life of our congregation. I stand on tiptoes, waiting for the movement of the Holy Spirit so these goals and dreams can be implemented—not that they are so far off but rather are within our reach. I believe the best is yet to come and that God has more work to do—not only for me but also for our congregation.

I also have some personal goals. I believe all of us as individuals ought to have some goals. Those begin with God. I want to become a better husband, father, grandfather, and servant; I want to work at becoming more disciplined in walking with God. I want to provide for my family's well-being so when the Lord calls me home to glory, my family will be secure, and I can leave something behind not just financially but also spiritually. I am blessed that I am able to begin a new era in the life of our family, from dropping out of high school and coming from a broken family, so that my sons and daughters, and those who will follow after them, will know I tried to leave a mark they could grab hold of and build on. I want to leave a good name they will never be ashamed of. It is important, particularly as a people of God, for us to leave footprints in the sand of time so our children and grandchildren will know that we walked with God and they are walking in our footsteps. They will be proud of their heritage and of their family so they can say, as the scripture records in Joshua 24:15, "But as for me and my house, we will serve the Lord". What a tragedy it is to wake up every morning and not have any goals or ambitions to look forward to. We see so much of that in our society, but my fervent prayer is that, as I wake up every morning, God will inspire me to do something for Him and His people. I have a saying that sits in my office (written by Michael Angelo) where I make my coffee every morning, and it speaks to my heart. It says, "Lord, grant that I may always desire more than I can accomplish." What a wonderful blessing that your heart's desire is to move beyond oneself to have goals and dreams that you are reaching for every day, and to know that God will give you the desires of your heart. I am confident, as I have listed several goals for ministry and my own personal journey that God will grant them to me. The goals may be lofty, and they may be high—in fact, they *are* high—but the God we serve is awesome and powerful. One of our deacons has a saying: "If our vision is so small, it may not be a vision at all." God does great and glorious things because He is a big God. I never in my wildest dreams thought I would be writing this book, engaged in ministry, and have a beautiful home and family, all because of God. He has been so great and glorious; He has actually blown my mind, done more for me than

I ever thought or imagined, and taken me to places I never thought of. I am still eager to see what God is going to do next.

I've just listed some of the things, but He knows the plans He has for me, plans to prosper and not fail. He has some things in store for me that I'm not even aware of. Whatever He has for me is for me, and I want to receive all He has for me. Let me add a disclaimer: His blessings aren't just for me but for all those who put their trust and hope in Him. This is just my little story, and the purpose of this book, as I indicated earlier, was never intended to be about me; it was purposed to get you to see what God is able to do.

We know there is no secret; what He's done for me He will do for you too. What He's done for many before me He will do for those after me. Just continue to look to Him for all you need and all you want to accomplish. Be daring enough to expect Him to do great things in your life. My accomplishments may be small to some, but they are big to me, for I know where I started, and I know where I am today. To God be the glory for all He has done for me and for many others like me. What an amazing God we serve. He never stops blessing us; He never stops empowering us; He never stops opening doors for us; and He never stops making ways for us, so dream big because we serve a big God. Establish high priorities and goals, and reach for them and have a deep determination to strive to be the best. Never try to compete against anyone; just be yourself and let God use you for who you are.

I stand in amazement when I look back over my life and see what the Lord has done. I praise Him every day for how awesome He is. Always remember that with God nothing is impossible; all things are possible with Him. Dream on, learn to set goals, and make a note when those goals are accomplished. Each time you reach a goal, give God praise and then set your sights on another goal. Make sure you remain humble and acknowledge who achieved that goal. When you are faithful over a little thing, God will bless you with much. It is hard for me to end this chapter because I am still pressing upward to new heights I'm gaining every day. Those are the words of a songwriter, but they are my words too.

Chapter 24

Falling in Love Again

I mentioned earlier that I have been privileged to write a monthly column for the *Philadelphia Tribune* and am grateful for the president and CEO of the oldest African-American newspapers in the country. Congratulations to the *Tribune* for having recently celebrated 130 years in existence. I grew up at a time when we had several African-American newspapers, yet many of them have been forced to shut down as a result of the economy, but the *Tribune* is still thriving. I wrote an article, published on Sunday, May 17, 2015, out of an experience I had. I have included the article, as follows:

> This was written as indicated as a result of a worship experience. I really want my marriage to finish strong, and am well aware of some missed opportunities I had to express that passionate love. God has blessed me with a wonderful wife and family, and I want God to know that I am appreciative that my passion for my marriage is as high as my passion for the church. After writing this article, I was told of someone who made tremendous financial gains in his career only to be saddened by missed opportunities resulting in the loss of his family. The person indicated that he would give all of his fortunes back if he could reclaim his family. How tragic it is that we spend so much of our time trying to gain success and fail to cultivate

and maintain our relationship with our loved ones. I've seen marriages of twenty or thirty years or more dissolved. They didn't dissolve over night, but they were not cared for. I have also seen the distance between children and parents as the result of them being absent in their lives. It is amazing how quickly our children grow; the days at the soccer or baseball field are few and romantic evenings with our spouses often become a thing of the past. I have observed couples and families when we go out to eat and see little or no conversation at the table, or in other instances I see the constant texting, or checking emails on their phone. The intimacy even at the dinner table no longer exists.

I sought to be transparent, open and vulnerable in this book and know that my marriage is nothing but the grace of God. I want God to know that I appreciate the gift of my wife. I never want to take any credit for our wonderful years of marriage for I know that it is God and God alone who granted us these meaningful years. I also deeply appreciate my family and grateful that they have loved me even during the times I was not there.

I remember celebrating our 25th wedding anniversary and we had the opportunity to renew our wedding vows along with other couples in our congregation. Again the words of my pastor ring in my heart, for he indicated he and his wife had been married over 50 years and that there were many exits along the way either of them could have sought, but they chose to remain together. The beauty is their marriage lasted for over 60 years and his devotion still rings in my heart. I am asking God not only to bless our marriage continually but that He might put a new surge, new energy, and new vitality in our relationship. I pray our golden years will be our best years and that my love will grow and glow; that the flame God has given me will burn brightly; that He will allow us to have many enchanting evenings together, and that my love is not simply expressed by the words I say, but rather by the heart I give.

I remember the words of a song that says, "love is better the second time around"; this is the second time around in the same marriage. When I say I am falling in love again, it is with the same woman that God has granted to me; with the same woman who has been by my side as first lady of our congregation; in love with the same woman who has been my partner, friend, confidant and lover as we raised our children and grandchildren; in love with the same woman who has been with me when I have not been the best of myself; the same woman who has been with me through my trials and troubles; the same woman who has been with me through my disappointments, failures, faults; and the same woman that I married until death do us part.

Prayerfully, these are not just my words, but words to those who are married or who plan to marry; that you will fall in love over and over each day and give God thanks for the beauty and sacredness of marriage.

Chapter 25

The Next Assignment

A s I conclude this book, I prayerfully hope it has been a source of inspiration to you. I am deeply indebted to our readers, for as I have said on many occasions, this project was never about me but always about God. I am well aware that others have started in the same manner I have or, for that matter, even in a worse situation; but let me repeat: it's not where you start but where you finish that counts.

Now let me say that I'm not finished; I am waiting for my next assignment from God. I know beyond a shadow of a doubt that God has some new opportunities, challenges, and assignments for me. I eagerly wait to hear from God so I may follow His footsteps. There is so much work to be done, and much of what you have read about is incomplete. I am looking forward to completing some of the things we started, but far more than that, I am looking forward to moving in a new journey. I am willing to walk by faith, trusting God all the way. We have just begun to see a glimpse of what it means to be a multicultural church. With all the turmoil and racial divide in our country and world, the church still stands as a symbol that we can be united by the blood of Jesus Christ across racial, geographic, and socioeconomic lines. I look forward to the home we have purchased, our Compassionate Home and Martin Luther King Jr. Gardens, to be a place where God's people are served.

I want God to continue to use me with energy, vision, and commitment so my latter days are my best days. I do not want to rest on my laurels or feel as though there is nothing else to be achieved. I feel I am ready for my next assignment for I have a frame of reference. I now know more than ever what God can do with a willing vessel. I have literally experienced the agony of defeat and the feeling of victory. I am able to look back and see how God has richly poured out His blessings on me, and I am yearning for more. I hear people say sometimes, "If the Lord doesn't do anything else for me, I am satisfied." I really can't say that; I can say He has done a whole lot for me, but I must admit I need more. When I wake up in the morning, I give God thanks for another day. I believe with all my heart that the best is yet to come.

God has enriched me, and every day I say to Him, "What is it You would have me to do?" There are many firsts in my life. This is the first book I have written; hopefully it won't be my last. I look forward to seeking to improve my writing skills. I want to expand our outreach ministry with television and radio ministries; I want to create a deeper environment where our church is known throughout the country as a place where we love God and serve people. I want to help shape and mentor the next pastor of this congregation and to be a mentor and coach for some of our younger preachers, in the same manner that my pastor, Reverend Dr. Albert F. Campbell, nurtured me.

I have been blessed to be able to share with some young pastors and preachers many of the experiences God has blessed me with. I share with them my strengths and weakness so hopefully they will gain some insight with respect to their ministry. One of the great blessings I received is to have the Reverend Dr. Alyn E. Waller, pastor of the Enon Tabernacle Church refer to me as his pastor. His father was called home to glory and the pastor who licensed him was also called home to glory. One Sunday morning when I was worshiping at the Enon Tabernacle Baptist Church, pastor Waller spoke to his congregation and shared from his heart that after much prayer and consideration he was led by the Lord to have me become his pastor. This young, gifted, dynamic preacher and pastor, bestowed this blessing upon myself. Dr. Waller is known throughout this nation, and for him to honor me in this way is more than I can even understand. I have a deep appreciation for his ministry and recognize that this honor is a gift from God. I truly value this relationship. God is amazing and I shall forever be indebted to God for blessing me with so many anointed servants that I cherish, sons and daughters in ministry and colleagues. God is stretching me.

I want to try something I never tried before, do something I never did before, explore some things I never did before, go to some places I never visited before, and step out into deep water where my faith can be stretched. I realize that the older you get, the more inclined you are to become fearful or complacent and willing to take risks; I want to be a risk taker for the rest of my life—not foolish risks but those that come from the voice of God. I want to help some youths experience the power of God in their lives; I want to really see the vision statement of our church embraced when we say, "The primary vision of our church is to develop a Christ-centered, multicultural church leading people to experience and cultivate a relationship with Jesus Christ. We seek to equip God's people for victorious kingdom living through proclamation, prayer, worship, teaching and fellowship."

This vision is embodied not only by those who are part of this congregation but also by the community in which we serve. I want to support our next president as I write these words, the first woman who will hopefully serve in the office of the president. I want to help cultivate and support political leaders in our community and city. I want to be a voice for the underserved and disenfranchised; I want to speak out for social justice. I want to continue to lead my family so my legacy can be imprinted in their hearts; this is for my children, grandchildren, and great-grandchildren, and for all those coming after me who will know I passed by this way. I don't want to quit on life or have life quit on me; I want to run the race every day with purpose in every step. I want my days and my life to count, and I want God to know He can trust me with an assignment. I'm not fearful, afraid, or intimidated; but I'm eagerly waiting to hear His voice.

I am confident that He isn't finished with me yet, and Lord knows, I'm not finished. I count it a privilege, an honor, and a blessing for Him to use me. I stand on tiptoes, waiting to hear Him say, "This is what I want you to do, this is where I want you to go, this is what I want you to say, this is where I want you to lead, or this is what I want you to follow."

Like Abraham, I want to not only know exactly where I am going but also know He has prepared the way. We walk by faith, not by sight.

No, the story hasn't ended; a new chapter is about to begin, and a new assignment is about to be given. I am ready, Lord. Use me for Your glory. I am ready, Lord. Make me a living vessel, renew me, restore me, refresh me, and count on me. I hear these words ringing in my heart and soul. Eyes haven't seen, nor have ears heard, what the Lord has in store. I will follow Him.

This is a marathon; I am going to run to see what the end may be. There may be some obstacles and roadblocks before I cross the finish line, but I want to finish, and I don't want to leave anything undone. I want to do all I can while I can. I have been blessed to be in the race; what joy has come to me. What fulfillment has been mine to receive. I can say I'm not tired yet; in fact, I have caught my second wind. I have been refreshed, I have been anointed, and I have been set apart for service unto God.

When you close this book, check us out on our website. Visit us at http://www.bbc4christ.org and see what assignment the Lord has given. In fact, I would encourage you to join me in the next assignment, for I know He has already prepared what I need, and you may well be a part of that assignment. Thank you again for sharing in this first part of my journey. Continue to hold me up in prayer that I may complete the task the Lord has given. Amen.

CPSIA information can be obtained
at www.ICGtesting.com
Printed in the USA
BVHW090802071222
653622BV00001B/122